Ancient Peoples and Places
SWITZERLAND

General Editor
PROFESSOR GLYN DANIEL

ABOUT THE AUTHOR

Born in Geneva in 1914, Professor Sauter studied and subsequently taught at the University of Geneva, becoming in 1949 Professor of Anthropology and Human Palaeontology, and in 1963 also Dean of the Faculty of Sciences. A former President of the Swiss Society of Prehistory and Archaeology, he has taken part in many excavations in Switzerland (mainly in the Valais) and in France, and in 1963 was appointed Cantonal archaeologist for Geneva. His many published works include general studies of Mediterranean prehistory and European races, as well as detailed surveys of individual Swiss cantons.

SWITZERLAND

FROM EARLIEST TIMES
TO THE
ROMAN CONQUEST

Marc R. Sauter

87 PHOTOGRAPHS
53 LINE DRAWINGS
9 MAPS

 THAMES AND HUDSON

THIS IS VOLUME EIGHTY-SIX IN THE SERIES
Ancient Peoples and Places
GENERAL EDITOR: PROFESSOR GLYN DANIEL

In memory of Emil Vogt (1906–1974)

First published 1976
© *Thames and Hudson Ltd 1976*

Filmset by Keyspools Limited, Golborne, Lancs.
Printed by Camelot Press Limited, Southampton.
Not to be imported for sale into the U.S.A.

CONTENTS

List of Illustrations

FIGURES

ABBREVIATIONS FOR THE ILLUSTRATIONS: MUSEUMS AND CANTONAL ARCHAEOLOGISTS

(see list of Swiss cantons)

ADGR	Archäologischer Dienst GR
BHM	Bernisches Historisches Museum BE
DAUG	Department of Anthropology, University of GE
HMSG	Historisches Museum SG
KAAG	Kantonsarchäolog AG
KASO	Kantonsarchäologie SO
KMSO	Kantonales Museum SO
KMUZG	Kantonales Museum für Urgeschichte ZG
LM	Landesmuseum (National Swiss Museum) ZH
M	Museum
MAHF	Musée d'Art et d'Histoire FR
MCAHL	Musée cantonal d'Archéologie et d'Histoire Lausanne VD
MCAN	Musée cantonal d'Archéologie NE
MSH	Musée zu Allerheiligen SH
RM	Rhätisches Museum, Coire⁄Chur GR

LIST OF SWISS CANTONS AND MAIN ARCHAEOLOGICAL COLLECTIONS

Canton (Half⁄canton)	Conventional sign used in the text	Collections
Aargau (Argovie)	AG	Aarau Brugg Baden Lenzburg

Aargau (Argovie)	AG	Seengen
		Zofingen
Appenzell		
1 Innere⁄Rhoden	IR	Appenzell
2 Aeussere⁄Rhoden	AR	
Basle (Basel, Bâle)		
1 Baselstadt (Bâle⁄Ville)	BS	Basle
2 Baselland (Bâle⁄	BL	Liestal
Campagne)		Augst
		Sissach
Bern (Berne)[1]	BE	Bern
		Biel⁄Bienne
		Délémont
		Thun⁄Thoune
		Herzogenbuchsee
Fribourg (Freiburg)	FR	Fribourg
		Bulle
		Estavayer
Geneva (Genève, Genf)	GE	Geneva
Glarus (Glaris)	GL	Glarus
Grisons (Graubünden,	GR	Chur⁄Coire
Grigioni)		Castaneda
		Scuol⁄Schuls
		Saint⁄Moritz
Luzern (Lucerne)	LU	Luzern
		Hitzkirch
		Schötz
Neuchâtel (Neuenburg)	NE	Neuchâtel
		Boudry
Sankt⁄Gallen	SG	Saint⁄Gallen
(Saint⁄Gall)		Oberriet
		Rorschach
Schaffhausen	SH	Schaffhausen
(Schaffhouse)		Stein am Rhein

Schwyz	SZ	Küssnacht am Rigi
Solothurn (Soleure)	SO	Solothurn
		Olten
		Dornach
Thurgau (Thurgovie)	TG	Frauenfeld
		Arbon
		Pfyn
		Steckborn
Unterwald		
1 Nidwald	NW	Stans
2 Obwald	OW	Sarnen
Uri	UR	(Altdorf)
Valais (Wallis)	VS	Sion⁄Sitten
		Brig⁄Brigue
		Saint⁄Maurice
Vaud (Waadt)	VD	Lausanne
		Avenches
		Château⁄d'Oex
		Nyon
		Orbe
		Vevey
		Yverdon
Zug (Zoug)	ZG	Zug
Zürich (Zurich)	ZH	Zürich (Schweiz.
		Landesmuseum,
		Musée national
		suisse)

Detailed information on the museums is contained in:
Cl. LAPAIRE. *Schweizer Museumsführer – Guide des musées suisses – Guida dei musei svizzeri.* Berne, Haupt, 2nd ed., 1969.

---

[1] A new canton, the Jura, currently being formed, has not been included because the exact boundaries are not yet known.

Preface

Fig. 1

As Switzerland is a small country it might seem easy to make a general survey of its pre- and protohistoric past, but for several reasons this is not so. Switzerland has an extremely varied relief which has resulted in a very diverse ethnic and cultural development. It is thus impossible to give an exhaustive survey and for each period the principal regions of the country will be distinguished: the Plateau, the Jura, the western and eastern Alps and their southern slopes which correspond to the zone of the Italian language (Tessin and the southern valleys of the Grisons).

The research and study of Swiss prehistory have been encouraged by the federalist system. Archaeology, as every science, is sponsored by the cantons. The advantage of this system has been to increase archaeological research and also the regional museums in addition to the Swiss National Museum. People are therefore fairly well informed and in some of the cantons they usefully pass on information. Local history societies often take an active interest in archaeology. Now seventeen out of the twenty-five cantons and half cantons have a local archaeologist. The Swiss Society of Prehistory and Archaeology also deserves praise for efficiently creating and encouraging interest in the prehistory of Switzerland.

Some regions are not yet well known, but this is being rectified. The large number of publications and the amount of museum material available makes the writing of a small book on the pre- and protohistory of Switzerland difficult. I have tried to present a text, not too overloaded with data, which will interest a wide learned audience while not being too condensed for specialists.

This book is not the first to deal with the history of Switzerland before the Romans. As early as 1901 J. Heierli presented a synthesis of what was then known on this subject; several works have also been published since then, and the principal ones are listed in the bibliography. The most recent work, *Ur- und frühgeschichtliche Archäologie der Schweiz*, vol. 4 (the Iron Age), was published in 1974.

I should like to acknowledge the help of the cantonal archaeologists and the museum curators, too numerous to mention, for supplying the photographs which illustrate the text. I am also grateful to the publishers who entrusted me with the task of writing this book, and to Madame Marthe Allain (Bourges) who accomplished the long and difficult task of translating the text into English, with the help of Barbara Rich and John Assias. My friend Dr Jacques Allain also deserves thanks for having patiently tolerated this time-consuming enterprise.

Fig. 1 Switzerland and neighbouring countries, showing environmental zones and political subdivisions.
1, boundaries between environmental zones (J, Jura; P, Plateau (Foreland); A, Alps); 2, state boundaries; 3, boundaries of Swiss cantons (for abbreviations see list pp. 11–13) and of the French departments, German länder and Austrian and Italian provinces; 4, cantonal capital

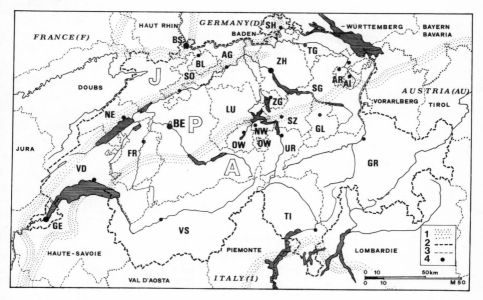

CHAPTER I

The Discovery of Swiss Prehistory

The history of archaeological research in Switzerland for the period up to the Roman conquest is characterized by several important stages. The first is the consequence of the rising interest among various people about 1830 in the exploration of caves and rock-shelters. Thus, in about 1833 François Mayor (1779–1854), a doctor from Geneva, discovered the Magdalenian sites of Veyrier (named after the nearby Swiss commune) in the vicinity of the Franco–Swiss border at the foot of Mont Salève. He mentioned, without attaching much importance to it, an engraving of a 'fallow deer' antler (in fact, reindeer) which is the first piece of *art mobilier* ever mentioned in the literature.

The most striking stage took place in the middle of the nineteenth century when, for several reasons, interest in national archaeology was developing widely. Firstly, the excavations – unfortunately superficial – undertaken in barrows and in other protohistoric structures brought to light a great number of fine objects (such as painted urns, bronze or gold vessels from the Hallstatt period). In this field the activity of Gustave de Bonstetten (1816–92) and Frédéric Troyon (1815–66) should be mentioned. Secondly, and most important, this was when lake-dwellings were discovered; the first was uncovered in 1854 at Obermeilen on lake Zurich, thanks to the initiative of a schoolmaster, Johannes Aeppli. On this occasion, the Zurich archaeologist Ferdinand Keller (1800–81) strengthened his international reputation by publishing his findings and stressing the importance of this type of site. His first report, *Die keltischen Pfahlbauten in den Schweizerseen* (Celtic pile-dwellings in the Swiss lakes), published the same year as the discovery, was followed by seven others by him and four more by J. Heierli and D. Viollier, etc. As early as 1862, Sir John Lubbock's essay on *The Swiss lake dwellings*, and then in 1866 J. E. Lee's English translation of F. Keller's reports (*The lake dwellings of Switzerland and other parts of Europe*), brought this new aspect of prehistory to the attention of the British public. F. Keller caused many Swiss and foreign amateurs to take up archaeology, including Colonel Frédéric Schwab (1803–69) at Bienne

BE, Dr Johann Uhlmann (1820–82) at Münchenbuchsee BE, Jakob Messikomer (1828–1917) at Robenhausen ZH, Professor Edouard Desor (1811–82) at Neuchâtel, and Dr François A. Forel (1841–1912) at Morges VD.

More will be said later about this enthusiasm for research in the Swiss lakes. This activity increased in western Switzerland between 1870 and 1875, following the 'correction of the Jura waters', which lowered the level of the Neuchâtel, Morat and Bienne lakes by two metres and revealed many new lake sites.

In 1858, as he was looking for lake sites, Colonel Schwab discovered the eponymous La Tène site (Marin-Epagnier NE); further investigations revealed the wealth of this great Iron Age culture.

Both the discovery and the excavation of the Upper Palaeolithic sites in the Schaffhausen canton (1873, Kesslerloch; 1874, Freudenthal cave) constituted a new stage and showed that such habitations did exist. Further investigations were successfully conducted in the Jura mountains and the Plateau.

Another aspect of the exploration of the Palaeolithic – the Mousterian – was revealed by investigations conducted early in the twentieth century in the Alps, with excavations by Emil Bächler (1868–1950) starting in 1903 at Wildkirchli, then at Drachenloch and Wildenmannlisloch. We shall see that the discovery of such an ancient culture in the middle of the Alps led several other investigators to prove its existence not only in other areas of Switzerland and neighbouring Alpine countries, but also in the Jura (for instance, Cotencher, Rochefort NE).

The beginning of the twentieth century was also marked by the publication of important reports: in 1901 Jakob Heierli (1853–1912), who was Ferdinand Keller's successor in Zurich, published *Urgeschichte der Schweiz* which is still a classic; while at Lausanne Alexandre Schenk (1874–1910) prepared the general study *La Suisse préhistorique* of which only the first volume, dealing with the Stone Age, was published (posthumously) in 1912.

The foundation in 1907 of the Swiss Society of Prehistory (Schweizerische Gesellschaft für Urgeschichte) emphasized the tendency for specialists and amateurs of prehistory to unite in their efforts to make the authorities and the public aware of the importance of their subject. The society not only deals with prehistory, but also interests itself in the archaeology of the Roman period and the Dark Ages, and has contributed to the spreading of knowledge of what the French call 'antiquités nationales'. In the beginning, it made up for the absence of courses in prehistory at Swiss universities which were slow to bring in the teaching of prehistoric archaeology. In 1905 Fribourg University gained distinction by inviting the young Abbé Breuil (1877–1961) to lecture, though not for long; the other Swiss colleges followed suit: in 1910, at Neuchâtel (Paul Vouga 1880–1939); 1916, at Geneva (Eugène Pittard 1867–1962); 1924, at Berne (Otto Tschumi 1878–1960); 1934, at Zurich (Emil Vogt 1906–74); 1961, at Basle (Rudolf Laur-Belart 1898–1972). This teaching supported the efforts made by several museums (among them the Swiss National Museum at Zurich founded in 1898) in scientific research, in the field and in the laboratory, into the remains of the pre-Roman and Roman periods.

In summarizing the development of prehistoric archaeological research in Switzerland many more people and sites should be discussed than space allows. Mention must be made, however, of a particular aspect of archaeological investigation in Switzerland, organized by the Swiss Society of Prehistory, namely the rescuing of sites threatened by motorways. Though these huge projects have concentrated mostly on Roman and medieval remains, they have also brought about important excavations at prehistoric sites, as at Auvernier NE (Neolithic and Late Bronze Age) since 1964. The same is true for the second great 'correction of the Jura waters' (1962–73), to which an archaeologist was assigned, which enlarged the channels between the lakes of Neuchâtel, Bienne and Morat.

GEOGRAPHIC CONDITIONS

Modern Switzerland is said to be 'Europe's turntable'. This was true long before tunnels were driven through the Alps. The country is divided into four zones. First, from south-west to north-east runs the

Fig. 1

Jura, a permeable limestone mountain range, most of which consists of parallel folds (the folded Jura) forming an obstacle nearly as impassable as the Alps, if not more so, because of the scarcity of river networks and therefore of easy crossing-points. The highest part of the range is over 1600 m. Its north-eastern limit lies along the northern bank of the river Aar. The tabular Jura, situated to the north-east, in the region of the

Rhine 'elbow' to the south of the Rhenan valley and the Black Forest, is not so high and is more dislocated, providing better crossings.

The second zone is the Swiss Plateau or Foreland, formed by Tertiary molasse seas deposits, those of the great circum-Alpine lakes, and finally by glacial moraine deposits which made up the Alpine ice-cap during the Pleistocene. The resulting relief created a dense water system in which the rivers, most of them belonging to the Aar and Rhine basins, flowed from south to north. This system is characterized from the Neolithic to the end of the Bronze Age by numerous lakes of all sizes; we shall see the important part they played in agricultural colonization.

At its south-west edge lake Geneva reduces the Plateau to a corridor. This plateau, with a minimum altitude of 350–400 m, is the most suitable area for human occupation owing to its fertile soil and its passage routes. There is a large corridor, opening widely to the north, which links the Danube, Rhine and Rhône basins. We shall often observe the part it played in the intermingling of cultural groups.

The Alps represent the most important of the four zones into which Switzerland is divided. The zone consists of the central part of the Alpine arc with its highest summits (Mont Blanc, 4810 m; Monte Rosa, 4634 m). But the height of this range should not give a false impression. This arc, with its spectacular peaks, is not a solid, impenetrable barrier. Indeed, it is cut deeply by the great river valleys flowing down from the natural reservoirs of the Gothard massif: the Rhône, forming the canton of Valais, and the Rhine – both longitudinal cuts; the Sarine, Aar and Reuss which open on the northern side towards the Plateau; and, to the south, the Doire, Toce and Tessin (Ticino), etc., which feed the Po.

These corridors are often linked, forming passes more or less favourable to human traffic. The most important of these passes, which were to play a great part at certain periods in prehistory, should be mentioned. Starting in the west there is first of all the Saint-Bernard pass (2469 m), which links the Piedmontese and Lombardian plains to the warm valley of the Rhône in Valais; it was presumably the first to be used. The Simplon pass is lower (2005 m) but is more difficult to penetrate and therefore does not seem to have played the same important role. In the Grisons canton there are the passes of San-Bernardino, Splügen, Maloja, Julier and Bernina, between 1800 m and 2330 m; they connect northern Italy to the Rhine valley.

We have not mentioned the Saint Gothard pass in the centre of this system. It is interesting to note that it was not opened till the Middle Ages, because of the extreme difficulty of access which was overcome only by the building of what was called, appropriately enough, the 'Devil's Bridge'. Only then was it possible for the transalpine traffic to take this most direct and shortest route, and for the inhabitants of the range to acquire a political significance which gave rise to the Swiss Confederation at the end of the thirteenth century.

The Alps are divided by a tight network of secondary valleys which are in turn access routes. The result is that this range, impenetrable at first sight, is in fact less difficult to cross than the Jura for much of its extent.

The fourth zone of Switzerland is made up of the southern slope of the Alps, mainly the Tessin canton, which includes the mountainous area and borders the northern edge of the Lombardian plain (lake Majeur, 193 m). Its southern climate gives it a character quite different from the other three zones.

Switzerland truly became the 'turntable of Europe' with the melting of the ice-caps, which opened up a diagonal passage the length of the Plateau and made the Alpine passes – essential to north–south traffic – accessible to man. The presence of so many points of access and transit routes turned Switzerland into a cross-roads open in many directions and leading to all major river basins. This meant that with wider horizons one could reach the Mediterranean through the basins of the Rhône and the Po (Tessin); through the Rhine basin one could find one's way to the great north European plain; while through the Danube basin one arrived in Central Europe and the Balkans.

The Pleistocene glaciers marked the Swiss landscape deeply, first by their formidable and sterilizing mass, then by their effects on the modelling of the earth in subsequent periods: the accumulation of deposits left by the melting glaciers which were then severely eroded; lakes in moraine amphitheatres and swamps turning into peat-bogs.

There is no need to discuss the number of Pleistocene glaciations since we are limited to those phenomena dealing with the prehistory of Switzerland. We need mention only the last two glacial maxima of Riss and Würm. During the widest extension of each of these two glaciations most of Switzerland was covered by ice-caps and glaciers; only the north-north-west part was unaffected. It is generally held that the maximum glaciation was that of Riss which left free only a small part of the northern Jura; this area was only open towards France and the valley of the Rhine north of Basle and also an area in the north of the Schaffhausen canton. At its maximum, the Würm glaciation not only came up against the Jura range but overlapped into the present cantons of Neuchâtel and Vaud; the area free from ice extended to Schaffhausen and into part of the Bernese Plateau as far as Napf, not to mention some secondary areas of lesser interest. A. Jayet has recently demonstrated that in the south-western zone of the territory the extent of the Würm glaciation was greatest, extending into the Rhône valley very near the present site of Lyon and covering the site of Geneva under 1000 m of ice.

Knowing the story of the last two glaciations one should not be surprised that the Palaeolithic period of Switzerland is limited to the cultures existing during the Riss-Würm interglacial (Mousterian) and during the regression phase of Würm (Magdalenian). One realizes also the extent to which the prehistory of a country is conditioned by glacial phenomena and their climatic consequences (variations in the limit of persistent snows, etc.).

From the point of view of the geological and chemical make-up of Switzerland and of its consequences regarding the degree and quality of the conservation of archaeological sites, one can make the following remark: the largest part of the territory is formed of limestone and is therefore favourable to such conservation. Crystalline zones are limited to the Alpine regions where ancient remains are more rare.

CHAPTER II

The Palaeolithic and Mesolithic

In Switzerland only two chapters of the long Palaeolithic period are known due to the Alpine glacial phenomenon. For the periods up to the Mousterian it is difficult to maintain that men would have avoided a territory which was probably as accessible and fertile as northern Italy or eastern France. The Riss glaciation, however, must have swept away most of the Lower Palaeolithic remains (Abbévillian and Acheulean) which could have been present in this area. What it did not destroy was buried under its moraines, greatly reducing the chances of our finding such remains, although a recent accidental find (1974) may contradict this. In a quarry at Pratteln BL, near the Rhine, a schoolboy found a flint hand-axe of Acheulean type. Though its geological position is not quite certain this object, which cannot be attributed to the Mousterian of Acheulean Tradition, testifies to human presence in the Rhine valley in Lower Palaeolithic times. It is not surprising that this tool comes from a region spared by Quaternary glaciers which obliterated other sites of the Mousterian, Aurignacian, Périgordian and Solutrean periods which lay in their path.

Plate 1

By chance some of the remains of Mousterian human occupation were situated above the upper range of these glaciers and so avoided destruction. There is also still hope that sites of this period will be discovered in the glacial region, provided that they are sealed in caves under a thin layer of moraine sediments, as was the case with the sites of Cotencher and Les Plaints in the Jura near Neuchâtel.

However, in our present state of knowledge, for the long Palaeolithic period there are only two stages of human occupation, alternating with the barren periods of the last two glaciations. First is the Middle Palaeolithic, the phase of Mousterian settlement, and second is the end of the Upper Palaeolithic with Magdalenian settlement, which ushers in the postglacial epoch.

MOUSTERIAN SETTLEMENT

Fig. 2

If, for the reasons stated above, we eliminate the Plateau and the Tessin from the distribution map of Middle Palaeolithic sites in Switzerland, we notice how scarce Mousterian settlements are. In fact, at present eighteen definite Mousterian sites are known, of which twelve are in the Jura and six in the Alps. This scarcity can easily be explained by the destruction and covering over of the land surface already discussed, and also by unfavourable geographic conditions.

On the one hand there is the Jura, with a relief which was and still is unfavourable for dense settlement. The geology of its ranges, made of anticlines and synclines unsuitable for the formation of a hydrographic system, can be added to a rather severe climate: even now, the temperature curve during the year at La Brévine NE (a high valley called 'Switzerland's Siberia') is similar to Moscow's. Thus it can be assumed that the Mousterians did not frequent these inhospitable mountains. On the other hand there are the Alps where it may seem surprising to find at such heights undeniable proof of the settlement – probably seasonal – of Middle Palaeolithic man.

The Jura

In the north of the country Mousterian sites are irregularly distributed. Most belong to the tabular Jura which was, as we have noted, more accessible. We must keep in mind that this area was spared to a large extent by the Riss glaciers, and completely by those of the Würm. In fact, four sites very near Basle – Münchenstein and Allschwil BL, Basle and Riehen BS – stand on the southern limit of the Rhine valley. These are open-air sites in the loess which are rather similar to those known in Alsace (e.g. Achenheim) and along the German Rhine (e.g. Oeflingen near Säckingen, Baden). Unfortunately the industry is very poor but the fauna is of interest (mammoth, woolly rhinoceros, cave hyena, etc.).

Three other sites are located in the basin of the Birse which flows into the Rhine at Basle. This region was favourable for the settlement of prehistoric man since there are a good number of natural shelters in the Jurassic limestone beds with easy access and where there is no water problem. The corridor-cave of Schalberg, near Aesch BL, crosses at 420 m the rocky ridge supporting the medieval castle. The fauna it contains is significant: the cave hyena predominates, not the usual bear. The industry is limited, indicating a hunting-site rather than a settlement. Kastelhöhle (Castle Cave, Himmelried SO), at 400 m, is a double rock-shelter which was first occupied during the Mousterian period,

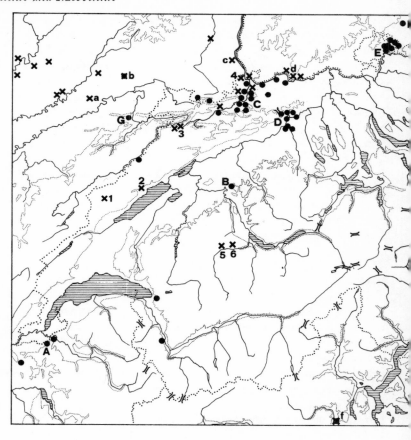

then deserted during the cold Würm maximum, and finally reoccupied during the Magdalenian period. The third is the little cave of Liesberg BE.

Entering the Jura towards the west we reach the Saint-Brais caves I and II, at an altitude of 960 m. They still belong to the Birse basin and therefore to that of the Rhine, though they are very near the Doubs, a tributary of the Saône and so directed towards the Rhône. In both these caves the presence of a layer of cave-bear bones and of a few quartzite

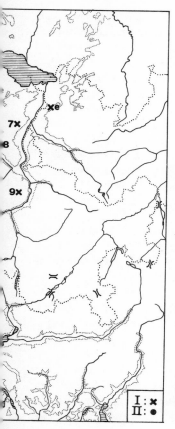

Fig. 2 Middle and Upper Palaeolithic sites. I, Mousterian; II, Magdalenian and Italian Upper Palaeolithic.
I: 1, *Couvet NE, Les Plaints; 2, Rochefort NE, Cotencher; 3, Glovelier BE, Saint-Brais; 4, Allschwil BL; 5, Oberwil BE, Schnurenloch; 6, Erlenbach BE, Chilchli; 7, Schwende AI, Wild-kirchli; 8, Selun SG, Wildenmannlisloch; 9, Vättis SG, Drachenloch. Outside Switzerland: a, Gondenans-les-Moulins F; b, Gonvillars F; c, Riedisheim F; d, Säckingen D; e, Koblach AU; f, Monfenera I; g, Erba I, Bucca del Piombo.*
II: A, *Etrembières F, Veyrier; B, Moosseedorf BE, Moosbühl; C, Valley of the Birse (BL, BE, SO); D, surroundings of Olten SO; E, Thayngen, Kesslerloch; Schweizersbild, etc. SH; F, Engen D, Petersfels; G, Villars-sous-Dampjoux F, Roche-dane. For sites b, f, g, see under Mousterian.*
Thin dotted line: 700 m altitude

implements is interesting, especially as in Saint-Brais II E. Koby discovered in 1955 the first remains of Mousterian man in Switzerland: an upper incisor which probably belonged to a Neanderthalian.

Some 40 km south-west of Saint-Brais is located the important Mousterian site of Cotencher (Rochefort NE). It is one of the most significant sites in Europe, not so much because of its archaeological characteristics as because of the fauna which was studied by H. G. Stehlin, the famous palaeontologist, who placed it in the Pleistocene period. The cave of Cotencher, 20 m deep, with a partly collapsed rock‑shelter in front, opens in the steep wall which forms the left (north) side of the Areuse gorges. This stream comes from the Val de Travers and flows into lake Neuchâtel. The cave, at an altitude of 659 m, overlooks the river Areuse for 130 m. It was occupied both by man and cave bears. The former could have hunted the bear but it is highly improbable that he was responsible for such a quantity of bones which represents, in the case of the bear, 95 per cent of the total of the collected bones. Sixty‑eight other species of vertebrates – among them forty‑nine mammals – make up the remaining 5 per cent. The variety of this fauna is astonishing, especially when one considers the ecology of the different species.

Besides ordinary species (lion, panther, wolf, Alpine wolf, bovines, red deer, horse) there are cold Alpine fauna (marmot, snow hare, chamois, ibex, etc.), Arctic fauna (polar fox, wolverine, lemming, reindeer, woolly rhinoceros, etc.), interglacial fauna (southern lynx), warm steppe species (Tartar fox, hamster), and two Mediterranean bats. This heterogeneity can be explained partly by the fact that these animals were brought into the cave (by man or birds of prey) when the climate was beginning to change with the Würm glacial advance, and partly because Cotencher is situated at an intermediate point between the cold valleys of the Jura and the well‑exposed southern side (where today lie the vineyards of lake Neuchâtel).

Fig. 3

The only remains of man's occupation in the cave of Cotencher is the flint assemblage which is mostly made out of a local siliceous stone of poor quality. There are also some other stones taken out of the moraine pebbles, as well as quartz rocks and a few flints from further afield. The designation Mousterian is suitable for the technique used to make these tools: the retouched flakes of classical type are relatively few but many others have 'pseudo‑retouch' made by involuntary crushing. A small number of tools have asymmetrical bifacial retouch. Some prehistorians have wondered whether two different industries are represented – one primitive and the other typically Mousterian – which had been mixed because of changes in the levels. Indeed, the lower archaeological level (brown layer), which was certainly much thicker at the end of the deposit, had been eroded and greatly altered during the advance of the Würm glaciation either by running waters or by solifluxion. It resulted in the upper level (level with pebbles) being the richest in tools. It is not

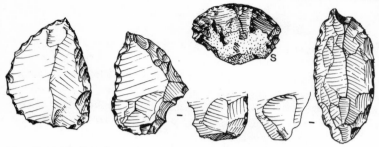

Fig. 3 Middle Palaeolithic; Rochefort NE, caves of Cotencher and Pfeffingen BL, and Schalbergfelsen (S); Mousterian flint industry. Max. length c. 6 cm

improbable that this erosion could have reached an original upper level which would have completely disappeared and thus produced a mixture. But such a phenomenon need not have occurred; the diversity of the material may reflect merely the heterogeneous character of the Cotencher industry, which can be compared with the so-called 'Charentian', the Mousterian of south-western France, which has a small proportion of tools showing the Levalloisian technique.

A few years ago a second site of the same type was explored by J. P. Jéquier: the cave of Les Plaints (Couvet NE), located about 13 km upstream at an altitude of 1080 m. Here he found fauna in which the bear was again the chief animal, and also several tools which are coarser than those of Cotencher.

Other similarities can be found further afield in the French Jura, for instance in the caves of Gondenans-les-Moulins (Doubs) and of Baume de Gonvillars (Haute-Saône).

The Alps
At the present time five definite Palaeolithic sites are known in the Alps. They are distributed as follows:
1. Eastern Switzerland: caves of Wildkirchli (Schwende AR), Wildenmannlisloch (Alt-St-Johann SG) and Drachenloch (Vättis SG).
2. Bernese Oberland (BE): caves of Schnurenloch (Oberwil), Chilchli (Erlenbach) and Ranggiloch (Boltingen). Of these three, we can disregard the Ranggiloch cave whose poor industry is certainly later than

the Mousterian. We can ignore two other sites, the cave of Steigelfad-balm (Witznau LU) at an altitude of 960 m and the cave of Les Dentaux (Villeneuve VD) at 1650 m, as we have no real proof of the presence of archaeological remains.

The most important site in eastern Switzerland is the double cave of Wildkirchli (Hermitage) which opens in the vertical walls of the Ebenalp in the Säntis range. Its lower entrance is at an altitude of 1477 m, its exit at 1500 m. Emil Bächler excavated it from 1904 to 1908 with the intention of collecting cave-bear bones but soon realized it was a prehistoric site. This induced Bächler to search elsewhere: he obtained interesting results at Drachenloch, 2445 m high, about 1500 m above the valley bottom (1917–23 excavations), as well as at Wildenmannlisloch which opens at an altitude of 1628 m in one of the rocky ridges whose upper edge forms the Selun summit which is one of the Churfirsten.

When Bächler's first discoveries became known prehistorians and Quaternary geologists were struck by this evidence of Palaeolithic man's presence in the Alps in glacial territory. To begin with some of them thought that the cave-bear hunters could have travelled over an ice-cap where the present Alpine summits emerge like the Greenland *nuna-takers*; thus, the caves would have overlooked an icy landscape. Further investigations into the way the cave strata were formed give a more precise idea of the relationship of the periods of occupation to the glaciations. The first point is clear: the three caves had not been reached by the Pleistocene glaciers. A complete analysis of the deposits, more especially of those from the archaeological and palaeontological levels, as well as an examination of the fauna and pollen, indicates that these levels were formed, like the similar brown layer of Cotencher, during the transitional period between the Riss-Würm interglacial and the beginning of the Würm glaciation. A sample of charcoal taken from a Drachenloch hearth, dated by C14, gave a date of *c*. 49,000 BC. The hunter of this period would have lived in an Alpine landscape where the glaciers played a more important part than today, though they were not an obstacle to his search for varied game (99 per cent cave bear; lion and cave panther, Alpine wolf, fox, ibex, chamois, red deer, marmot, snow hare, etc.).

Apart from traces of hearths and a slab at Wildkirchli which Bächler interpreted as a work-unit, archaeological evidence consists of quite good quality tools made of quartzite and others of siliceous rocks (hornstein, radiolarite, etc.). The raw material was probably brought into the caves as it is not found there naturally. As at Cotencher there are many flakes with broken edges and real tools are scarce. There are various scrapers and blunt points. The Levalloisian technique is present if not common.

Archaeologically speaking, Drachenloch is exceptional. There is no tool assemblage of the same type found in the other two caves, though Bächler interpreted a few calcareous flakes as crude points. Man's occupation in this high altitude site is attested only by traces of a hearth.

The results of Bächler's research in the Alpine sites gave rise to two controversies – one concerning the possibility of a bone industry, the other concerning the existence of a 'bear cult'.

Bächler maintained that there was no doubt about the bone industry. A good number of cave-bear bones were broken at certain points and some (1 out of 1000) are polished. Their distribution in the cave is irregular, with no polished bones at all in one area and in another a pile of bones of the same type. Particular bones of the skeleton have clearly been selected: mostly long bones, hip-bones and mandibles; canines are also frequently worn down by polishing. Today, however, we are very sceptical about the possibility of proving that Palaeolithic man of the Wildkirchli group tried to make tools by breaking bear bones (Bächler thought they were used in skinning hides). Polish visible on some of the bones could be explained by natural causes, for instance what Koby called 'charriage à sec', i.e. pressure exerted by bears on bones left on the ground which made them break at the weakest point; they pushed the bones around and into the cave floor, thus driving them into the earth and rubbing projecting pieces. It is difficult, therefore, if not impossible, to distinguish between a bone subjected to such natural actions and one which was deliberately broken and used by man. However, it is not really a question of a tool assemblage, as the simple fact of breaking a bone does not make a tool. Further observations in carefully excavated sites of the Lower and Middle Palaeolithic might indicate the occasional use of naturally broken bones.

The problem of a 'bear cult' is more delicate. Indeed, it is based on Bächler's observations, made in good faith, at Drachenloch. There, he said, he ascertained the presence of several special deposits, the most spectacular of which was an accumulation of seven cave-bear skulls, with their mouths orientated towards the cave entrance and surrounded by a kind of box made of thin stone slabs (inner dimensions 0.95 × 0.90 × 1 m) and covered by a larger slab. Nearby there may have been deposits of bear skulls on slabs, an accumulation of long bones between the cave wall and a low wall made of small slabs, etc. After eliminating the natural causes and the utilitarian reasons (such as meat deposits), Bächler concludes they are ritual deposits. In his monograph (1940), he presents a detailed argument based on numerous ethnographic parallels and concludes in favour of a 'bear cult'. The idea was received favourably and was disseminated widely by ethnologists.

Since then a more cautious attitude has had to be adopted. Bächler unfortunately failed to use certain essential archaeological methods during his excavations at Drachenloch. He excavated very rapidly, progressively destroying all that he found without trying to leave the most important structures *in situ* for others to see. In addition, he took no photographs, drew no plans and kept no accurate records. His successive publications show that he drew the box with the seven bear skulls from memory. The peculiar characteristics of the cave may also have misled him. It was hollowed out by corrosion of the rocks, of which the most important is limestone. The horizontal limestone strata easily break up into slabs, so that the sections fallen from the roof and walls are numerous in the clay deposit, where they often form mounds which might easily resemble low artificial walls. As for the orientated skulls and long bones of the bears, detailed observations made in other caves of the same period (for instance, Les Furtins, excavated by A. LeroiGourhan) have shown that natural or perhaps even human causes (at least unconscious) might explain such an assemblage: the bear or man walking in a passage tends to throw aside what is in his way; moreover, the slow slipping of the clay carries the bones and may deposit them at certain points (holes, obstacles). In conclusion, we cannot accept Bächler's statements at Drachenloch as a basis upon which to build farreaching theories concerning a 'bear cult'. We must hope that future excavations in another cave (not yet discovered) will allow the problem to be reconsidered on a new basis.

The three caves of Appenzell and SaintGall are of great interest. Bächler's excavations gave rise to investigations in the whole of the Alpine arc and above all in Switzerland, where three serious amateurs from Berne, D. and A. Andrist and W. Flukiger, systematically explored the caves and the rock-shelter of Simmental in the valley of the Simme, the Bernese Oberland river which flows into lake Thoune. The discovery of several Palaeolithic and Mesolithic sites was the reward for their long and difficult work. Two of these sites are of interest to us here: Schnurenloch (1230 m) and Chilchli cave (1810 m). We cannot detail all the characteristics of the two sites, but the many stratigraphic and palaeontological analogies with the caves of the Jura and of eastern Switzerland should be noted.

Plate 2

In the fauna of Schnurenloch the presence of musk-ox (represented only by a single phalanx) is unusual. The stone industry is very poor: twenty small flakes in the lower level of Chilchi are of Mousterian type, but three out of four from Schnurenloch were obtained by the Levalloisian blade technique.

Taking together all the facts observed in the five Alpine sites attributable to the Mousterian, we may recall that they were occupied by hunters of bear and other species during quite a long period between the end of the temperate climate of the Riss-Würm interglacial and the first stages of the Würm glaciation. They made tools out of rocks from various sources, using techniques utilized elsewhere in Europe at the time, the Levalloisian technique being the least frequent. They may also have used naturally fractured cave-bear bones without their being deliberately fashioned as tools. Probably only a few Mousterians came to the caves, employing them as hunting sites. The idea that they practised rites in connection with hunting must be abandoned in view of the lack of precise and proven facts.

It is still not known to which human type these hunters belonged. The only tooth from Saint-Brais, though it seems to belong to a Neanderthaloid, does not permit a more precise definition.

Switzerland does not have the only Alpine Mousterian sites. Quite a number have been investigated in the French Alps, for instance the cave of Baré (Onnion, Haute-Savoie, at about 1190 m); in the Vercors range the cave of Prélétang (Presles, Isère) at 2000 m and the cave of Eugles (Saint-Laurent-du-Pont, Isère) at 850 m; and farther south, the cave of Fournet (Solaure, Drôme) at 1200 m and the site on the river terrace of Bas-Guillotte (Buis-les-Baronies, Drôme). The Mediterranean area, of which H. de Lumley published a general survey, need not be mentioned. In the Italian Alps Mousterian levels are known in the caves of Monfenera (Borgosesia, Piedmont) at 665–75 m. The Mousterian is also found in the Monti Lessini and the foothills of the Alps north of Vicenza. In the Austrian Alps there are some doubtful remains between the Rhine and the upper valleys of the Traun and the Enns in Styria (cave of Salzofen, Bad Aussee, and of Liegl, Tauplitz). Farther east in the same province, Drachenhöhle at Mixnitz (950 m) and the cave of Repolust at Peggau (525 m) should be mentioned. The link with the Mousterian of the Slovenia mountains (Mornova zijalka, at 520 m, etc.) is thus clear. All these sites demonstrate that Mousterian man was attracted by the game and other resources offered him in the Alpine valleys.

The advance of the Würm glaciers to their maximum left its mark on the hunter as well as on the whole nature of the area we are studying. It was not until the ice-caps retreated that the conditions necessary for human life returned. The wait was a long one, lasting almost 400 centuries (1400 generations), before man in Switzerland could venture to cross the areas which had become passable again: this is the period of Magdalenian settlement.

MAGDALENIAN SETTLEMENT

According to processes which are still not fully understood, *Homo sapiens neanderthalensis* gave way during the Würm glacial maximum to *Homo sapiens sapiens* and his variants (Cro-Magnon, Combe-Capelle, Chancelade). Concurrently the Middle Palaeolithic Mousterian was superseded by the cultures of the Upper Palaeolithic: the Lower Périgordian (or Chatelperronian), followed by the Aurignacian, Upper Périgordian (or Gravettian), Solutrean and finally the Magdalenian. Remains of these cultures have been found in countries bordering Switzerland, particularly in France.

Fig. 2

In the present state of our knowledge it seems that Switzerland first became habitable again during a late phase of the Magdalenian. The question has often been asked whether there was an earlier occupation, perhaps of Gravettian type, during an as yet undefined phase of the Aurignacian. The only indication which would support such an hypothesis is the poor and atypical lithic industry found in an upper level at Saint-Brais I; but this is not enough.

We must, therefore, restrict ourselves to the Magdalenian. The environment was characterized by the sub-Arctic climate of the late glacial phase, marked by the after-effects of the last glaciation: a cold and dry climate interrupted only twice by more temperate oscillations – the Bölling and Alleröd. The cold pressures are named after the typical Alpine plant, the Dryas (Oldest, Older and Younger Dryas). The glaciers had retreated into the valleys. In central Switzerland, for example, a terminal glacier was present on the Vierwaldstättersee. In the moraines left by the melting ice lakes formed, of which the smallest became peat-bogs, and a whole hydrographic system developed; thus, the Plateau took on its characteristic features.

On the newly freed ground a thin layer of vegetation grew up which increased slightly during the Bölling interstadial and especially during the Alleröd, with small trees (birches and dwarf pines, willows and bushes, sallow-thorns) related to the steppe and the tundra. The fauna associated with this climatic and plant milieu was the typical one for the period. Reindeer was the chief game animal along with the hare and snow partridge. Though some of the species known elsewhere, such as the saïga antelope, were absent in this area, the Plateau was frequented by the wild horse, bison, aurochs and, less frequently, the musk-ox, woolly rhinoceros and mammoth. The ibex was more common than the chamois, which is surprising since the latter is now present on the Plateau. The Magdalenian hunters killed polar foxes, lynxes, wolverines and brown bears.

The Magdalenian settlement, taken as a whole, was confined mostly to the north and west of Switzerland. In the north there are three concentrations of sites: the Schaffhausen canton; the area of the Birse basin and Rhine elbow; and the central Aar valley and Olten region. In the west the sites are isolated and dispersed: in the Jura near Neuchâtel (Bichon cave, La Chaux-de-Fonds NE); on the Plateau, the open-air site of Moosbühl (Moosseedorf BE); and in the Alps, perhaps the site of Schnurenloch in the Simmental (Oberwil BE) and the rock-shelter of Scé du Châtelard (Villeneuve VD). The site of Veyrier, located in the French commune of Etrembières (Haute-Savoie), close to the Swiss commune of Veyrier GE, is usually included in the Swiss sphere.

The most important sites are those of Schaffhausen and Veyrier. Unfortunately they were poorly excavated and the finds collected there are scattered in many museums. It is especially regrettable since in two of the sites there was a sequence which could have indicated the stages of settlement of these people. Kesslerloch (Thayngen SH), like Schweizersbild a few kilometres away, was densely occupied, and it is estimated that more than 32,000 flint tools were collected from the two sites. In addition, there is a rather important reindeerantler industry. There are weapons: javelin points of different kinds, harpoons with one or two rows of barbs. One harpoon found at Kesslerloch is unique: it gives the impression of imitating a harpoon whose barbs would have been tiny flint points, fixed by a binding indicated by an engraved motif. There are spearthrowers, arrowstraighteners, needles and a semicircular bead (Kesslerloch), etc.

One of the most attractive aspects of the two Schaffhausen sites is the presence of objects of *art mobilier* which have become classics of their kind. Horses and reindeers are engraved on arrowstraighteners (among them the famous reindeer, thought for a long time to be grazing, but which is more likely a male smelling out its rival's track) or on lignite plaques, and there are sculptured artifacts (mostly throwers), among them a protome of a muskox. This very fine art belongs to the late style IV of the chronology proposed by A. LeroiGourhan. The characteristics of the industry clearly indicate that these sites belong to the latest stages of the Magdalenian. However, the first occupation of Kesslerloch may have been slightly earlier.

The Rhine and the Jura have about twenty Magdalenian caves or rockshelters. Among others, there are Kohlerhöhle (Brislach BE), Kastelhöhle (Himmelried SO), Brugglihöhle (Nenzlingen BE) and Hollenberg (Arlesheim BL). They have revealed, besides a sometimes varied cold fauna, a flint industry of local origin; bone and antler tools are seldom represented. Noteworthy as special finds are a tooth for suspension from Hollenberg in the form of a schematic female figure of the same kind as the one in the German cave of Petersfels not far from Schaffhausen, and a piece of a harpoon with a double row of barbs from the Heidenküche shelter (Himmelried SO).

Around the town of Olten, located on the Aar, are terraces of the folds of the Jura. The Magdalenians settled on several folds, either under rockshelters or upon rocky terraces. The first type of dwelling is found at WinznauKäsloch, Mühleloch (StarrkirchWil) and Sälihöhle Oben

Plate 3

Plate 4

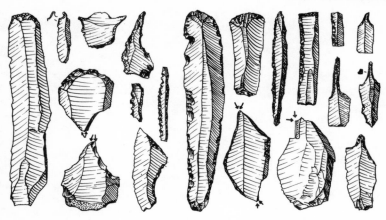

Fig. 4 Upper Palaeolithic; Moosseedorf BE, Moosbühl; Magdalenian flint industry. Max. length c. 9.5 cm

(Olten). The second type is found only at Hard I and II, which overlook the railway station of Olten, and Köpfli (Winznau SO). Apart from the sites of Winznau, these sites are poor and their interest is due mainly to their geographical situation. Farther west, in a small cave at Oensingen SO, a piece of bone with an engraved ibex was found in 1973. Farther south the open-air site of Moosbühl has some topographical conditions similar to those of Meiendorf and Stellmoor in northern Germany: a low moraine ridge emerging from a peat-bog. The analogy stops there, however, as this site has revealed only a flint industry; traces of dwellings are difficult to interpret, and it is hoped that new excavations – now in progress – will give a more typical picture of this site which is unusual in Switzerland.

Turning briefly to the Alps, one can point out the presence of a flint bladelet in Schnurenloch cave, whose stratigraphical position makes one assume that a Magdalenian hunter ventured into this mountainous area during the principal advance of the Würm glaciation; but this single find is weak evidence.

At the site of Scé du Châtelard (Villeneuve VD), at the upper end of lake Geneva, the only evidence known so far of Magdalenian occupation is two scrapers, some reindeer bones and a human metacarpal. It has

Plate 5

Fig. 4
Fig. 5

35

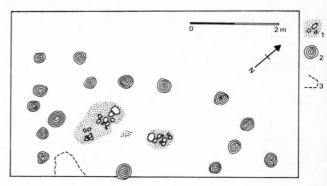

Fig. 5 Upper Palaeolithic; Moos-seedorf BE, Moosbühl; plan of part of a Magdalenian shelter, with post-holes. 1, hearth; 2, post-hole; 3, disturbed zone. Redrawn after H. Schwab, JBHM, 1969–70.

the advantage of giving a point of reference for the retreat of the Rhône glacier at this period.

The Veyrier sites (Etrembières, Haute-Savoie F) have an exceptional setting. The wall of Mont Salève, whose strata are vertical on the north-west side, partly fell down at the end of the Quaternary, presumably on to the remains of the local Arve glacier. On the surface of the fallen rocks boulders piled up, forming with the gravel and soil small rock-shelters in which the Magdalenians settled. The shelters were situated at an altitude of 450–500 m at the foot of a cliff, and overlooked the basin of Geneva whose lake was 30 m higher than today. Investigated rather carelessly during the nineteenth century after 1833, these sites revealed many lithic and bone implements. A few interesting pieces of art were also found, including an arrow-straightener with an ibex and plant motif, and a curious object whose interpretation has not been agreed upon: some people think it is a harpoon with a double row of lateral barbs, but according to E. Pittard it is a ramiform sculpture as the barbs are orientated towards the point. We shall reconsider below the remains of human skeletons found at this site.

From an archaeological point of view the Magdalenian of the Schaffhausen–Veyrier region belongs to a late stage of its evolution. Its connections with the Magdalenian of south-west France have been shown, but since recent work on the many migrations of Palaeolithic reindeer the idea has been rejected of a transhumance that could have drawn the hunters from the Dordogne or the Pyrenees to Schaffhausen.

The obvious similarities between certain artifacts of the Schaffhausen area and corresponding ones at Ariège or Périgord can be explained by the slower movements of human communities, independent of the migratory oscillations of the reindeer. Other affinities with Central Europe have been suggested. Feustel tended to connect Moosbühl with the German group of Oelknitz (or Döbritz) and to distinguish a 'Thayngen group' including, among others, Brugglihöhle, Winznau-Köpfli, Kohlerhöhle and, in southern Germany, Petersfels. This idea was not accepted by Mrs D. de Sonneville-Bordes who thinks that 'the conquest of the Swiss territories seems to have been undertaken by populations of a homogeneous civilization; the first advance post to be occupied being, without doubt, Kesslerloch'. This conquest would have been one of the consequences of 'the sudden and extensive human expansion' which characterized the Magdalenian in south-west France. The theory is a highly plausible one.

In the region under review we know Magdalenian man's physical type from an incomplete skeleton in the Bichon cave (La Chaux-de-Fonds NE) and a small series of remains at Veyrier. Unfortunately, none of these bone fragments were excavated under good conditions; nevertheless there are sound reasons for dating them to the Palaeolithic. It is interesting to note the racial diversity of these men. If we oversimplify, we recognize Cro-Magnon features in the man of Bichon (though he might have been rather short) and in the remains of Veyrier 2. The skeleton from the site of Les Grenouilles (Veyrier 1), which shows a healed depression in the right parietal section and a well-knitted oblique fracture of the left tibia and fibula, is more difficult to classify as the face is absent; it could be related to the Chancelade type. Finally, a very broken skull (Veyrier 3) has an obvious resemblance to Combe-Capelle man. This anthropological variety proves that the Magdalenian groups in Switzerland and neighbouring territories often moved around and intermingled.

THE MESOLITHIC – THE LAST HUNTERS

For some years now a more complete picture has been emerging of events in Switzerland between the end of the true reindeer Magdalenian and the first Neolithic settlement (*c*. 8000–3500 BC).

The Palaeolithic and Mesolithic

The Alpine glaciers would not have been different in extent from those of today. This means that the climate was then at an optimum, reflected in both the vegetation and fauna, although there were one or two minor cold oscillations of little significance. During this very temperate stage, starting with the Pre-Boreal and Boreal periods and becoming more marked during the Atlantic period, a type of sediment was deposited (red earth), at least in western Switzerland in the Rhône basin, which could not have formed under other climatic conditions.

At a poorly defined moment during the Late Mesolithic hunters did indeed go up into the Alps, for their traces have been found in Simmental (BE), Ranggiloch (1845 m) and Chilchli cave (1810 m), not to mention Oeyenriedschopf (Diemtigen) (1180 m) and the Riedli shelter (Zweisimmen) (950 m), lower down.

The composition of the natural vegetation of the landscape changed gradually. During the Pre-Boreal (8000–6800 BC) a mixed pine/beech forest was predominant; this was superseded during the Boreal (6800–5500 BC) by a forest of pine and hazel, which itself gave way to the mixed oak forest of the Atlantic phase (5500–2700 BC). The natural vegetation provided a suitable environment for Mesolithic man. It was only towards the end of this period that the forest began to restrict his movements, thereby encouraging the fragmentation of cultural groups.

The fauna, without the previous Arctic species, was much the same as that which existed almost to the Middle Ages. The game animals in greatest demand were wild boar and red deer. The marmot, chamois and even the ibex may well have persisted in the Jura.

Fig. 7

The living places of the Mesolithic hunter were very varied. Rock-shelters continued to be occupied, especially in the Jura (Birse district, the Roches Pass NE, Baulmes VD) and in the Alps (Simmental BE). The only shelter on the Plateau, Baume d'Ogens VD under a molasse cliff, belongs to this type. All the other Swiss Mesolithic sites are in the open, on the banks of rivers or small lakes. Up till now, they have only been found in the centre and the north of the Plateau, between the lakes of Bienne (BE-NE) and Pfäffikon ZH; most of them are identified by hundreds of flakes collected in the fields year after year by patient investigators. In two of these sites (Schötz LU and Wetzikon ZH) there were simple huts made of light material, close to pits. At Schötz LU there was a workshop for making antler tools.

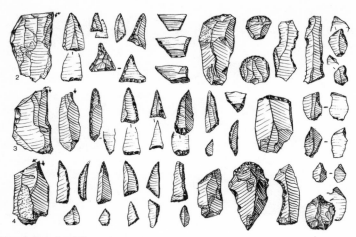

Fig. 6 Epipalaeolithic and Mesolithic; Nenzlingen BE, Birsmatten rock-shelter; flint industry from levels 4 and 3 (Sauveterrian) and 2 (Tardenoisian). Max. length c. 3.5 cm

The evolution of the Mesolithic can be summarized very schematically as follows, according to R. Wyss's tentative classification.

The Magdalenian tradition continues in the form of an Epipalaeolithic, known mainly from the open-air site of Fürsteiner (Seeberg BE), not far from the lake of Burgäschi which has become famous for its Neolithic lake-dwellings. The site dates back to 8250 BC, just a little later than the Magdalenian site of Moosbühl BE which is only 20 km farther south. A few changes in the inventory of stone implements (no awls, rarity of large blades, a small quantity of multiple tools) are the sole indicators of development between the two periods.

The evolution continues with the progressive introduction of geometric elements (especially triangular microliths), accompanied by microburins; they are found at Schötz LU and Wetzikon ZH. This transformation seems to be further accentuated by the arrival from the west during the seventh millennium BC of bearers of a culture related to the Sauveterrian. This is the case, for example, in the lower levels (5–3) of the small cave of Birsmatten (Nenzlingen BE) on the Birse, and in the levels of the shelter of Cure at Baulmes VD, at the foot of the Jura, as well as at the site of Baume d'Ogens VD (dated to *c.* 6700 BC). Microliths increase, while small backed points, on the other hand, grow rarer.

Fig. 6

39

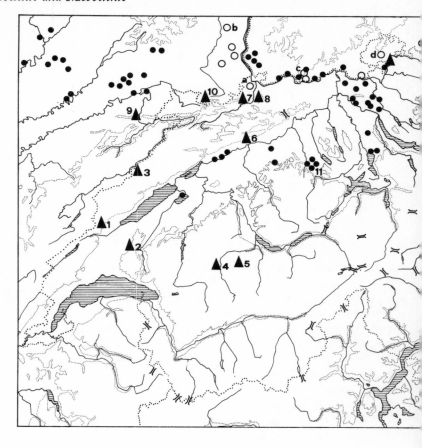

Plate 6

About the middle of the early Atlantic period (5000 BC) a change occurs which can be linked with Tardenoisian influences coming from the south-west. The flint industry now has trapezoidal arrowheads with transverse edge, Tardenoisian points and notched blades. The bone and antler industry becomes more important: perforated axes, picks, holders, chisels and above all flat harpoons with wide perforated or notched bases. These harpoons, found in a good stratigraphic position especially at Schötz LU and Birsmatten (Nenzlingen BE) levels 2 and 1, are

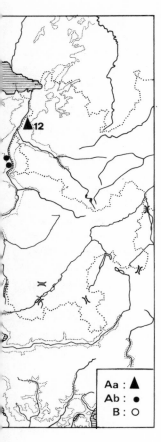

Fig. 7 *Epipalaeolithic, Mesolithic and Early Neo-*
lithic sites. A, Epipalaeolithic and Mesolithic (a,
rockshelter; b, open-air site); B, Early Neolithic:
Linear pottery.
A: 1, *Baulmes VD, Abri de la Cure;* 2, *Ogens*
VD; 3, *Le Locle NE, Col des Roches;* 4,
Zweisimmen BE, Riedlibalm; 5, *Diemtigen BE,*
Oeyenriedschopf; 6, *Balm bei Günsberg SO;* 7,
Nenzlingen BE, Birsmatten; 8, *Arlesheim BL,*
Birseck; 9, *Villard-sous-Dampjoux F, Rochedane;*
10, *Oberlarg F, Mannlefelsen;* 11, *lake of Wauwil*
LU; 12, *Koblach AU.*
B: a, *Bottmingen BL;* b, *Mulhouse F;* c, *Säckingen*
D; d, *Gächlingen SH;* e, *Singen D.*
Thin dotted line: 700 m altitude

important as they demonstrate beyond doubt that they are not connected
to the Azilian cultural group.

The Late Mesolithic follows with its numerous, generally trapezoidal
geometric microliths, unguiform scrapers and absence of burins. It is in
the Fällanden horizon that the Neolithic techniques and forms
(arrowheads with flat retouch) slowly appear. This 'Neolithization'
increases after 4000 B C when the trapezes disappear and the microliths
lose regularity; small axes present indicate the process.

Plate 7

It is difficult to draw a chronological distinction between the last true Mesolithic and the genuine Neolithic. Birsmatten level 1 (Tardenoisian) has produced a radiocarbon date of 3400 B C, very close to that of the first Neolithic settlement. It is highly probable that groups of hunters led the same Epipalaeolithic and Mesolithic way of life even when the first Neolithic influences were beginning to be felt in the Plateau.

Among the most interesting cultural elements of the Swiss Mesolithic can be noted the occurrence of roughly painted pebbles in the small cave of Ermitage at Birseck (Arlesheim BL) not far from Basle. Unfortunately it is impossible to identify precisely the level in which they were found, as the layer was not separated from the Magdalenian deposit.

Apart from a few fragments of human bones excavated at Baulmes VD, only one reliable skeleton has been found belonging to the Swiss Mesolithic: the male skeleton from Birsmatten (Nenzlingen BE). Unfortunately this precious evidence, discovered during illicit excavations, cannot be attributed with certainty to level 3 (Sauveterrian) or level 2 (Tardenoisian). The man appears to be a typical descendant of the Upper Palaeolithic, and can be linked with the Cro-Magnon type except for the height, which is about 1.60 m, perhaps less.

CHAPTER III

The First Farmers

When speaking of the boundary between the Mesolithic and the Neolithic we have suggested that groups carrying on the hunters' tradition coexisted with other groups bearing the new culture. The transition between the two ways of life has many different aspects. As proof there are the conclusions drawn recently from the site of Abri de la Cure, near Baulmes VD at the foot of the Jura. The Neolithic layer (Middle Neolithic, 3000–2500 BC) follows with hardly a break a level defined as Late Mesolithic containing trapezes of Tardenoisian type. This latter layer has wild fauna but also cereal pollen. If the presence of these cultivated crops were actually to prove not to be due to intrusion by burrowing animals, then this layer should no longer be called Mesolithic but pre-pottery (or aceramic) Neolithic. This would be the first appearance of the pre-pottery Neolithic in Switzerland, dating back to 4000 BC. It is possible, therefore, that Switzerland gradually underwent a process of Neolithization before one can speak of a real Neolithic culture and period. It is interesting to note that the first element of the new culture is also the most fragile and the most strongly linked to climate: that is to say the cultivation of cereals and of those plants which are indigenous only in the Near East and nearby European countries such as Greece. It is still too early for us to say by which route and in what manner this innovation penetrated into the northern Alps.

SWITZERLAND AS A CROSSROADS

The geographical position of Switzerland adds great interest to the question of which routes were taken from the Near East by the bearers of the new culture. There are two main possibilities, indicated at a great number of sites. On the one hand, there is the eastern continental route via the Balkans and the upper Danube basin. On the other hand, there is the southern sea route, probably for coastal trade, along the northern Mediterranean coasts. The former route brought the Danubian cultures to Central Europe, characterized during their final stages by Linear ware. The second possibility is less easy to trace, but is responsible for the introduction, at the mouth of the Rhône, of the culture characterized by impressed ware. These two currents pass both sides of the Alps.

THE MIDDLE NEOLITHIC

The chronological classification of the Neolithic is not easy. Theoretically it should be established by taking into account the whole Neolithic period in all the Eurasian and North African territories. But this would only result in categories which would be too large to be useful. The opposite solution consists of dealing only with a restricted area, as Paul Vouga did intentionally around 1930 when he interpreted the stratigraphic sequences which he uncovered in the lake-dwellings of lake Neuchâtel; he distinguished a 'Néolithique lacustre ancien', a 'Néolithique lacustre moyen' and a 'Néolithique lacustre récent'. We have adopted an intermediate formula, following the scheme put forward by Alain Gallay. It deals with western Europe – thus also with Switzerland – and distinguishes first an Early Neolithic, characterized by highly individual cultures (Mediterranean cultural groups with impressed ware in the south, Linear pottery groups in Central Europe). At this stage (before 4000 B C), Switzerland is still in the Late Mesolithic period, with the possible exception, as stated above, of the Baulmes site.

The Middle Neolithic follows in which the specific features of the two main currents mentioned earlier change and influence each other to a varying degree according to the region. At this moment, groups appear to become different and the process of cultural mixing increases particular aspects: ethnic-cultural groups, local features, etc. Besides, it is not always possible to locate their origins. In western and southern Switzerland lies the Chassey-Lagozza-Cortaillod complex. The first covers nearly all of France, the second, parts of northern Italy, the third extends slightly over the present Franco–Swiss border. In the north and east, but mainly in southern Germany, there are groups which are directly derived from, or which were influenced by other secondary currents, with stylistic variations allowing cultures to be distinguished both in space and time (especially in the case of Linear pottery). Among the Central European groups may be mentioned those which might have played a part in the formation of the Swiss Middle Neolithic period: the groups of Altheim and Aichbühl, Rössen, Pfyn and

Michelsberg. Some other related groups extended eastward and northward into France, where they developed individual characteristics according to the extent of their contact with the Chassean.

What is the Middle Neolithic in Switzerland? The first culture distinguishable from the Mesolithic tradition is that of Egolzwil.

The Egolzwil culture This culture is unfortunately known from only one site – Egolzwil 3 – located north-east of the ancient lake of Wauwil LU, now dried up, which was already an area of Mesolithic settlement. Here a group is present which definitely specialized in the growing of crops (wheat and barley) and the breeding of domesticated animals (mostly goats and sheep, pigs and a very few cattle). The absence of dogs may be due to chance. Nevertheless, hunting supplied an important part of the food intake (about 57 per cent). Farmers established themselves successfully in a site situated on the banks of the lake which had recently emerged following a lowering of the water-level. On the banks a thin layer of vegetation had begun to appear. Here the settlers built wooden houses directly on the damp ground, putting a covering of large flat layers of oak bark, with their outer surfaces upwards, between themselves and the earth. Thus, it is not a site of pile-dwellings but rather of shoreline structures with vertical posts sunk deeply into the soft ground. The presence of a fence on the side facing away from the lake also shows the 'terrestrial' character of this Egolzwil 3 village.

The pottery made at the site is of good quality but there is no great diversity of shape and decoration. The principal types are large round-based vessels with two, three or four handles on the sides; when they are decorated, it is in a discreet way, with several small lugs or notched lines. Among the non-ceramic industries, wood-work is important and has been well preserved by the moist earth. Especially noteworthy are the beautiful hafts for polished stone axes, carefully shaped from the lower part of young ash trees; the part which held the axe was widened in order to weigh down the tool. Sickle handles extended into a kind of spindle into which a flint blade was set obliquely; there are also containers.

An important factor for the relative chronology of Egolzwil 3 and its connections with the Danube is the presence of a few vessels originating in the late 'Linear' group known as the Rössen. The C14 date for the site (*c.* 2900 BC) fits well with the date of the late Rössen culture (*c.* 3000 BC). The particular features of Egolzwil 3 are not easy to connect with

Fig. 8

Plate 8

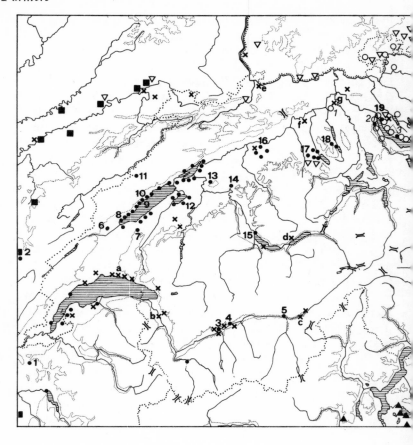

other cultures, as they do not have much in common with the Danubian complex and their relationship with the groups of Mediterranean origin is not clear. It has been proposed that Egolzwil 3 is a local result of the Neolithization of a Mesolithic community; thus the main influences would be rather that of the Mediterranean current. Egolzwil 3 is the first site to show the results of this influence. There are no guide lines to record the Mesolithic evolution which it had to pass through. Indeed, farther west, the evidence is rather different.

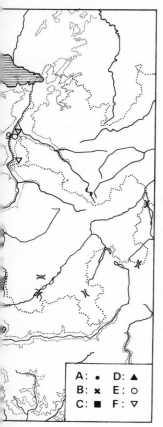

Fig. 8 Middle Neolithic sites. A, Cortaillod and kindred cultures; B, graves of Chamblandes type; C, Chassey culture; D, Lagozza and Square-mouthed pottery cultures; E, Pfyn culture; F, Rössen group.

A: 1, Frangy F, Malpas; 2, lac Chalain F; 3, Sion VS; 4, Saint-Léonard VS; 5, Rarogne VS; 6, Baulmes VD; 7, Chavanne-le-Chêne VD, Vallon des Vaux; 8, VD; 9, Saint-Aubin NE; 10, Cortaillod NE; 11, Le Locle NE, Col des Roches; 12, Greng FR; 13, Sutz BE; 14, Moosseedorf BE; 15, Thun BE; 16, lake of Burgäschi BE/SO; 17, lakes of Wauwil LU, Egolzwil and Schötz; 18, Hitzkirch LU, Seematte; 19, Zurich, Gr. and Kl. Hafner.

B: a, Pully VD, Chamblandes; b, Collombey-Muraz VS, Barmaz; c, Glis VS; d, Niederried BE, Ursisbalm; e, Arlesheim BL, Birseck; f, Däniken SO; g, Lenzburg AG.

D: a, lake of Varese I.

E: 1, Lenzburg AG; 2, Zurich, Bauschanze; 3, Meilen ZH; 4, Gachnang TG, Neiderwil; 5, Pfyn TG, Breitenloo; 6, Steckborn TG; 7, Thayngen SH, Weier; 8, Sipplingen D; 9, Eschenz FL, Lutzengüetle.

Thin dotted line: 700 m altitude

The Cortaillod cultures   As early as 1929 Paul Vouga identified in his stratigraphic excavations of the Neuchâtel lake-dwellings a lower layer to which he gave the name 'Néolithique lacustre ancien' in his classification of the lake-dwelling Neolithic. Emil Vogt was to widen this concept to the whole of Switzerland, giving it in 1934 the name 'Cortaillodkultur'. In 1949 Miss V. von Gonzenbach undertook a synthesizing study of this culture and also gave this name to it. But since then many discoveries and numerous studies have been made. They have resulted in the interpretation of the Cortaillod as a complex of local groups and stratigraphic, thus chronological, levels: hence the name Cortaillod cultures. It is out of the question to list them here. We will merely give a general definition of the complex before mentioning some of its aspects.

Most of what we know of the Cortaillod complex comes from the lake-dwellings. These are found from lake Geneva to lake Zurich, including the lakes of Neuchâtel (the richest), Morat, Bienne and Thoune, not to mention the small expanses of water of Lobsigen and Moosseedorf BE, Burgäschi BE + SO, Wauwil, Sempach and Baldegg LU. Along these lake shores the Cortaillod farmers built their villages in a similar fashion to Egolzwil 3 but with certain differences, as for

Plate 9

instance in the way the floor and hearths were constructed. The houses always had a wooden frame fixed into the soft ground, supporting a roof which probably had two sloping sides and walls constructed in between, made of closely set poles. The whole structure was covered with rough-cast clay; the roof was presumably thatched. It seems that there was generally only one room. The hearth was most often made of clay which was periodically renewed to avoid the rising damp. The houses were

Plate 10

clustered into small villages, though not one of them has ever been entirely excavated. It is therefore impossible to know how many units formed the complex. There is one exception: the southern site at the small lake of Burgäschi (dating back to *c.* 3000 BC). Here a rectangular area (50 × 12 m), stretching along the bank and fenced in on the other three sides, contained two houses (the largest approximately 10 m in length) and an enclosure for cattle with a shed. It is therefore really a family farm rather than a hamlet. Relying upon statements from well-excavated sites, it is possible to estimate that a village comprises between ten and twenty houses.

Other types of dwellings are reported, however, the two most significant of which are clusters on rocky hills, and camps in caves and rock-shelters. The most characteristic examples of the former are located in the Valais canton, at Saint-Léonard and Rarogne. Here two small communities had built their huts on the loess soil which used to fill up the holes in the rocky mounds which rose out of the flanks of the mountain. At 50–100 m they dominated the alluvial plain of the Rhône, which was once a marsh. As for the rock-shelter sites, the most

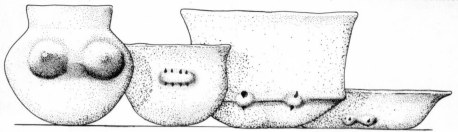

Fig. 9 Middle Neolithic; lake Neuchâtel Cortaillod culture; pottery. 1–3, Saint-Aubin-Sauges NE, Port-Conty; 4, Onnens VD. Max. ht. c. 20 cm

striking is that of Vallon des Vaux (Chavannes-le-Chêne VD), located on a narrow natural shelf half-way up a marl and molasse cliff. However, sites also exist on the plain, as at Petit-Chasseur, Sion VS.

The communities which gathered in these different types of settlement were all farmers – more so than at Egolzwil 3, with several varieties of wheat, barley and millet – and shepherds (with dogs). By putting together the evidence from seven lake-dwelling sites of this period we find that 48 per cent of the animals are domestic, but this average hides a considerable variability (about 15–74 per cent).

The specific Neolithic techniques are already fully developed. Pottery is characterized by good quality clay, the surface of which is carefully burnished from black to reddish beige. The forms are varied but round bases predominate. The proportions and the vessel sections have a chronological and ethnic significance, as we shall see below. Another technique which appeared during the Neolithic (along with basket-making which had been known since the Mesolithic) is flax-weaving. It is attested at this time mainly by weaver's implements and it developed rapidly. Unfortunately no Neolithic loom has yet been discovered; it was certainly a very simple device which could weave only rather narrow strips, with the warp made taut by clay weights.

Plate 11, *Fig. 9*

The hard-stone technique is unremarkable. The polished-stone axes are of a simple type though there are a few perforated hammer-axes. Flint-working provided knives, scrapers, diverse points (a point-scraper is typical) and arrowheads which are always more or less triangular. Antler and bone were used extensively as they were in the other Neolithic cultures. Among the special features of Cortaillod may be

49

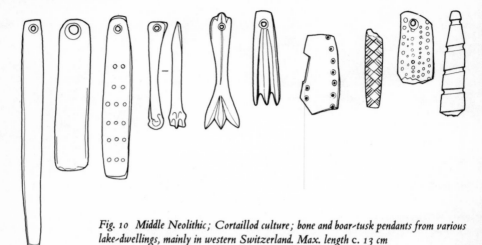

Fig. 10

Fig. 10 Middle Neolithic; Cortaillod culture; bone and boar-tusk pendants from various lake-dwellings, mainly in western Switzerland. Max. length c. 13 cm

mentioned the axe-haft of the simplest type and elongated pendants, perforated at one end and sometimes decorated with geometric patterns, and others made of antler divided by circular grooves. Boar's tusks were often shaped and polished to be made into personal ornaments.

Among the so-called Cortaillod cultures it has been possible to distinguish chronological and regional groups. Recent excavations (Zurich, Auvernier NE, for instance) will certainly lead to a more precise delineation of these groups. Some of the groups are known from several sites rich in implements, mainly along the lake shores between the lakes of Pfäffikon and Geneva. The culture can be recognized in nearby France at lake Chalain (Jura) and near the Rhône (Génissiat, Ain; Chaumont-Malpas, Haute-Savoie). The pottery presents greater variety: along with simple jars there are many carinated vessels, often decorated with horizontally or vertically pierced lugs. The carination sometimes has an extension which makes it look like a circular blade which may or may not be perforated. There are plates, lamps, bowls, some with a very wide rim. Decoration also becomes diversified: geometric patterns incised before or after firing, lugs placed in various ways under the rim or on the carination, cords with multiple vertical perforations, etc. A type of decoration confined to the late Cortaillod culture may be noted: it consists of applying patterns cut out of birch-bark to the neck of the vessel, whose white colour contrasts with the black base of the resin which was used for glue.

The Vallon des Vaux group   This group in the north of the canton of Vaud (Chavanne-Le-Chêne-Vallon des Vaux and perhaps Baulmes) appears to be the result of the blending of late Cortaillod with the other cultures of the Chassey-Cortaillod-Lagozza complex.

Plate 12

The Saint-Léonard group   This group is restricted to the canton of Valais (Collombey-Barmaz, Saint-Léonard, Rarogne-Heidnischbiel), and is mainly located in the Rhône valley. Most of its assemblage is related to late Cortaillod but in addition there are, on the one hand, elements of foreign origin (for instance, pottery decoration of Chassean type), spindles and one sherd of a square-mouthed vessel, from northern Italy, on the other hand, original pottery forms and decorations such as deep grooves and vertical cords on the girth. In connection with the environment it may be mentioned that flint had to be imported and so the first Neolithic people in Valais substituted other materials. Along with hard stone and bone, they found quartz in their mountains: it was difficult to work but produced beautiful tools.

Plate 13
Fig. 11

In 1974 the discovery at the hill of Saint-Léonard VS of a rock with cup-marks and petroglyphs, related to those of Val Camonica which E. Anati assigns to a period contemporary with the Middle Neolithic, raises very interesting questions. Could the connections be proved, it would support the idea of links between the inhabitants of Saint-Léonard and those of northern Italy.

Fig. 12

Fig. 11 Middle Neolithic in the Alps; Saint-Léonard group; Saint-Léonard VS; typical pottery; max. ht. 30 cm (top right: spindle-whorl of Lagozza type; diam. c. 6 cm)

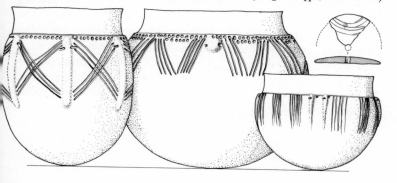

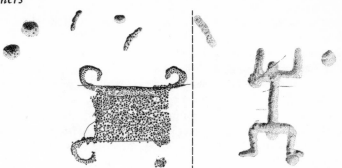

Fig. 12 Neolithic and Early Bronze Age in the Alps; Saint-Léonard VS, Crêt des Barmes; examples from a complex of rock engravings. Anthropomorphic figure: Middle Neolithic; engraving at left: Early Bronze Age. Ht. of figure c. 32.5 cm

The Dickenbännli group In northern Switzerland, between the valleys of the Aar and of the Rhine between Basle and Schaffhausen, there are sites, generally not well excavated, which present very special features. The absence of pottery does not make their attribution easy. These sites yielded mainly flint implements, including triangular arrowheads and very thin points (the so-called Dickenbännli type), the use of which is unknown. It might be that this is the result of acculturation by a Mesolithic community, unwilling to accept pottery but adjusting its lithic equipment to a new way of life, under the influence of the late Cortaillod farmers.

Burials We must now discuss an aspect of the Cortaillod cultures which has only recently been brought to light, namely the burials. It has generally been agreed that one can attribute crouched inhumation, mostly in stone cists, to this group of cultures. This custom has been known for some time and named the Chamblandes type, after the oldest known cemetery at Pully near Lausanne VD. What made the cultural classification of the burials difficult is the scarcity and monotony of their grave-goods: boar tusks sometimes arranged in the shape of a pectoral (?), shaped, polished and perforated Mediterranean shells, flaked flint axes, triangular arrowheads, etc. Pottery is very rare.

The cemeteries of this culture lie along the Rhône, from the southern part of the French Jura (caves of Souhait, Montagnieu, Ain) to the valley of Conches in the Upper Valais, not far from the source of the river, passing by both banks of lake Geneva – mainly the Riviera between Lausanne and Montreux VD – Collombey, Sion, Glis near Brigue (VS). This geographical distribution is completed by a succession of points on the Plateau (and in the upper valley of the Aar) down to lake Zurich. In this area the most important site is at Lenzburg AG where a burial complex has recently been investigated in detail. Among the particular features of the cemetery it can be noted that one of the tombs contained the skeletons of fourteen individuals and that several children's graves were grouped together under one stone paving (parts of the tombs can be seen in the Swiss National Museum in Zurich). It should also be stated that the Lenzburg cemetery has produced material which does not entirely belong to the Cortaillod culture but rather to one of those cultures of Danubian or northern origin. This proves that burial rites are less tightly bound to one culture than certain technological and artistic features. But on the whole the distribution of the Chamblandes cists is quite similar to that of the Cortaillod cultures. The Valais cemeteries are obviously connected by the Great Saint-Barnard pass with those of the Aosta Valley (Montjovet, Villeneuve, Vollein, etc.) which are in turn linked to the north Italian culture of Lagozza.

In the Valais canton there is another expression of man's religious beliefs in the Middle Neolithic: the line of standing-stones or 'menhirs' – some of them decorated with dotting – discovered at Sion not far from the site of Le Petit-Chasseur. They were buried under the deep alluvial deposits of the river Sionne; it is at least likely that these monuments

Plates 15, 16
Fig. 13

Fig. 14

Plate 14

Fig. 13 Middle Neolithic in the Alps; Saint-Léonard group; Collombey-Muraz VS, Barmaz II; cemetery of cists. Small numerals indicate height above 440 m

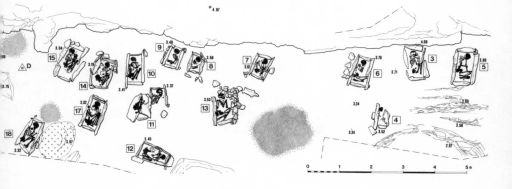

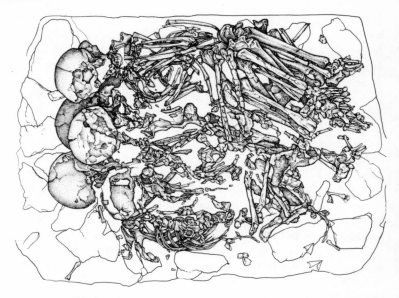

Fig. 14 Middle Neolithic; Cortaillod or Pfyn culture; Lenzburg AG; interior of a grave with six bodies. Length of grave c. 1.10 m

belong to this period. Finally, at Petit-Chasseur in a layer of the same period, masks shaped from sheep skulls were found in two refuse pits of a house. It is reasonable to think that they were used originally for religious purposes.

Cultures from east and north While this relatively homogeneous Cortaillod cultural complex was developing, the eastern and northern parts of the Jura, the Plateau and the Alps were under pressure from groups from southern Germany and even farther afield. Here again only the most typical of these groups will be discussed.

This is the period of the slow incursion of the early Linear pottery culture from Central Europe. In fact, the culture was only noted at a few sites in northern Switzerland and it is connected with the secondary centres of the Rhine area between Alsace and lake Constance. One may imagine small communities of primitive farmers penetrating into a territory still occupied by the first settlers who were carrying on their

Mesolithic hunting and gathering way of life; from them the farmers borrowed more than one implement.

It is no wonder, therefore, that the Schaffhausen canton to the north of the Rhine should present several sites belonging to this infiltration of agriculturists looking for land easy to cultivate, and for loess in particular. But this influence is mainly felt a little later, at the time of the Rössen culture, when pottery had become more evolved and complicated. Such pottery has been found around lake Wauwil (Egolzwil 3, Schötz 1) and in Zurich. Sherds of the same type have been noted as far away as Valais (Saint-Léonard).

Michelsberg and Pfyn Until 1960 a parallel was drawn between the Cortaillod culture in north-eastern Switzerland and a Michelsberg culture, the distribution area of which lay mainly on the Rhine, from Alsace to Westphalia. Since J. Driehaus's investigations, a group known as the Pfyn culture has been separated from the Michelsberg culture, and this new group is located almost exclusively in north-eastern Switzerland, between lake Zurich, the Schaffhausen canton and the western part of lake Constance, with an isolated branch in the principality of Liechtenstein. Among the most important sites of this group are Weier (Thayngen SH), Breitenloo (Pfyn TG) Egelsee-Niederwil (Gachnang TG) and Sipplingen (Ldkr. Oberlingen, Württemberg, Germany). These are generally lake- and moor-dwellings. The two most important Weier levels were dated by C14 to between 2600 and 2500 BC.

The pottery of both the Pfyn and Michelsberg cultures has a few round-based forms, others with a flat base, as well as a tulip-shaped beaker. Most flat-based vessels are characteristic of Pfyn; some are decorated with a thick, rough and uneven slip. Another more artistic ornament consists of a thickened rim with a row of small arcs cut into the lower edge. The presence of a triconical footed bowl suggests the influence of eastern Central Europe.

Plate 17, *Fig. 15*

The lithic equipment is closer to the Cortaillod culture than to the Michelsberg; arrowheads are varied in shape. There are quite a number of well-made perforated axe-hammers (Michelsberg axes); the most beautiful could have been imported. Ornaments made of bone and teeth are more diversified than in the Michelsberg culture and are very likely the result of contacts with Cortaillod.

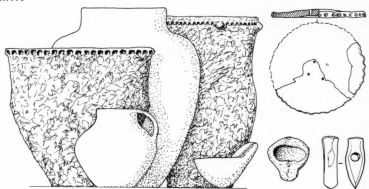

Fig. 15 Middle Neolithic; Pfyn culture; coarse and fine pottery. Top right: 'bread plate' (or lid?); bottom right: perforated stone axe-hammer. From Pfyn TG, Breitenloo, Thayngen SH, Weier, Wetzikon, Robenhausen and Weisch ZH. Max. ht. c. 48 cm.

Metal, in the form of copper, was to a limited extent part of the Pfyn cultural inventory. Some implements, especially small crucibles, demonstrate not only the presence of imported objects but also the knowledge of smelting and working of this metal, thanks to the influence of more highly advanced Central European cultures.

Pfyn represents a localized cultural entity whose origin is still disputed. Its affinities with the Altheim culture, which overlaps the German Danube upstream from Ulm, are clear. We have already mentioned connections in the north-west with Michelsberg on the Rhine and Cortaillod.

It is interesting to note that the Pfyn culture, unlike the Cortaillod, does not seem to have penetrated the Alpine zone; in any case, the site of Eschen-Lutzengüetle FL is the farthest point away on the Rhine, located on the way out from the mountains. The colonization of the Alpine basin of the Rhine would only take place during the next stage (Horgen, Early Bronze Age).

THE LATE NEOLITHIC

Around 2500 BC an important change occurred in Switzerland as well as in the northern and western Alps. It was not a revolution, because the farmers and stock-breeders continued the same way of life. It was rather a

Fig. 16

matter of new cultures taking the place of a previous one. It would be premature to speak of the replacement, thus of the elimination, of one ethnic group by others; indeed, we do not believe in such processes since it is not easy to wipe out a whole population, even a relatively small one like that of the Neolithic. Instead, we should imagine the arrival of a few alien groups, settling among the indigenous people. They could have been persuasive and enterprising enough to impose their culture without disturbing the economic traditions of the others. It has been possible to demonstrate in one or two places (for instance in the Auvernier NE lake-dwelling) that the Cortaillod culture gradually became a part of a new culture, in this case, the Horgen culture. But we must confess that nothing is known of the processes of acculturation at work during prehistoric times.

The Horgen culture   In the middle of the third millennium B C the first of the new immigrants appear in the lake-dwellings, in levels separated from those of Cortaillod and Pfyn by a layer of archaeologically sterile lacustrine clay. It is generally held that these immigrants came from northern France and that their culture was derived from the Seine-Oise-Marne culture (abbreviated: S.O.M.). This relationship raises many problems but it is difficult to find another origin for the Horgen culture. According to Marion Itten, who has taken up the question again, one Horgen group deriving from an ancient stage of the S.O.M. culture probably settled on the Swiss Plateau, mainly around lakes Zug and Zurich but also between these lakes and the Rhine. From there the traits of this new culture could have spread westwards to lake Neuchâtel, northwards to south-western Württemberg, east and south-eastwards into the Rhine valley, upstream from lake Constance, and penetrating the Alpine area (site of Cazis-Petrushügel GR) on the Hinterrhein at a height of 748 m.

The Horgen culture is not as rich and varied as Cortaillod and Pfyn. The ceramic industry was clearly in a state of decline. Instead of the fine   Plate 18, *Fig. 17* and well-burnished pottery with various profiles and shapes, there appear vessels with a monotonous appearance, made of coarse clay usually containing a coarse-grained temper; the walls are thick and the surface is generally uneven. The base is always flat. Decoration is poor: a groove under the rim, irregular lines, a row of dots and a few knobs or lugs. There are, however, some rare examples of figure decoration:

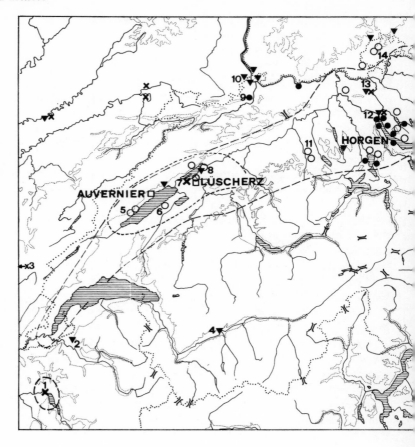

anthropomorphic motifs made of dots which are new in Switzerland. It is extraordinary to think that the tradition of beautiful Middle Neolithic pottery could have disappeared to be replaced by such poor quality ware.

The remainder of the material culture is less specific. Polished-stone axes are rectangular in form. They were held in place by an antler haft of a new shape, with a winged projection firmly fixed to the head of the haft. In addition there are perforated axe-hammers. Flint was the material used for blades, points, scrapers, leaf-shaped daggers, and well-

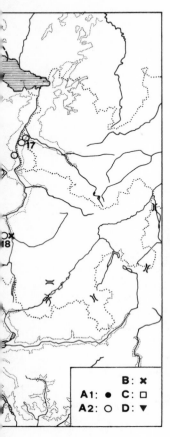

Fig. 16 Late Neolithic sites. A, Horgen culture: boundary indicated by long dashed line (A1, early stage; A2, late stage); B, Corded-Ware culture; C, Auvernier-Lüscherz groups: boundary indicated by thin dashed line; D, Bell-Beaker culture.
1. Annecy F; 2, Cranves-Sales F; 3, lac Chalain F; 4, Sion VS, Petit-Chasseur; 5, Concise VD, La Lance; 6, Chevroux VD; 7, Fénil-Vinelz BE; 8, Sutz and Lattrigen BE; 9, Pfeffingen BL, Schalberg; 10, Allschwil BL; 11, lake of Wauwil LU; 12, Zurich, many lake-dwellings; 13, Schöfflisdorf ZH, Egg; 14, Wilchingen SH; 15, Eschenz TG, Isle of Werd; 16, Sipplingen D; 17, Koblach AU; 18, Cazis GR, Petrüshugel. Thin dotted line: 700 m altitude

made arrowheads, which were generally triangular as before, more rarely lozenge-shaped or with a wide tang.

Ornaments are not very distinctive; there are a few pendants made of stag antler and some small flat pebbles perforated near the edge. Metal-working is represented only by a coarse small copper blade of a dagger (Meisterschwander AG). This scarcity is all the more striking as it follows a more important series of copper tools and ornaments in the Cortaillod and Pfyn cultures.

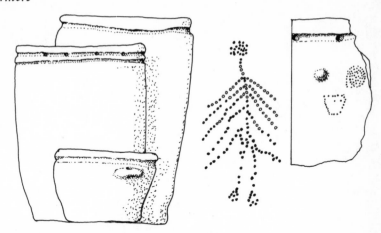

Fig. 17 Late Neolithic; Horgen culture; pottery from Zurich-Utoquai (max. ht. 42 cm) and anthropomorphic and animal figures on pottery from Meilen ZH and Eschenz TG (ht. of figure c. 17 cm)

Three-quarters of the Horgen culture sites are located on the edges of lakes and marshes. The most important ones are: on lake Zurich, several sites in Zurich itself (Rentenanstalt, Wollishofen and Utoquai), at Horgen and at Meilen ZH; on lake Bienne, Lattrigen BE; on lake Neuchâtel, the sites of Saint-Aubin/Port-Conty NE. In Germany on the western shores of lake Constance are located the sites of Sipplingen, Bodman and Wangen.

Fig. 18

We know little about the burial rites practised by the people of the Horgen culture. Though it is not altogether certain, we may assign to these people a ruined dolmen at Aesch BL, the Pierre Percée at Courgenay BE – a slab with a hole in it ('Soul's hole'), all that remains of a large dolmen. A small dolmen at Laufon BE and one at Auvernier NE could possibly belong to the same people, as might the vestiges of three dolmens in south-west Germany: the Heidenstein ('Heathen's stone') at Niederschwörstadt near Säckingen, the Toter Mann (the 'Dead Man') at Degernau, LdKr. Waldshut and the Sinkelosebuck near Altenburg. It is surprising to note our relative ignorance of Horgen burials, considering the links that connected this culture with the French S.O.M. culture; indeed in the latter we are aware of the importance of the megalithic tomb (gallery-grave) and of the hypogeum. This could be explained (as G. Bailloud has suggested) by the fact that the Horgen culture may have developed from an early stage of S.O.M. when these prestige burials did not yet exist.

What happened south-west of the Swiss Plateau while the Horgen culture was developing is little understood. It seems that this culture evolved into regional variants, two of which have recently been distinguished and are being analyzed: the Lüscherz group and the Auvernier group. Both are present in Switzerland especially around the lakes of Neuchâtel, Bienne and Morat. The Lüscherz group (from the lake-dwelling of Lüscherz or Locras BE on lake Bienne) might have been formed earlier and its development could be partially contemporary with that of Horgen. It is characterized by round-based vessels with a simple decoration of dots under the rim.

As for the Auvernier group, it covered a larger area centred on the Jura, and seems somewhat more recent (Auvernier NE, *c.* 2000 BC). It retained the most typical shapes of Horgen pottery – coarse cylindrical vessels – but beside these were vessels whose origin has not yet been ascertained. Finally, more than one vessel is related to the corded-ware which characterizes the culture bearing this name. The hard-stone axes are worthy of note: indeed, they were not made in the same way as all the other Neolithic axes (i.e. by patient wear and polishing) but by the flint-flaking technique. Only the cutting edge is polished. The flint itself was imported for the first time. Beautiful implements (daggers, knives, tanged arrowheads) were made of the dark to light-brown flint from Grand-Pressigny (Indre-et-Loire F). Provided no other sources of flint of the same quality are discovered, it must be acknowledged that trade relations existed at this time between the central producer of good quality flint and Switzerland.

The Corded-Ware culture   This culture, which was partly contemporaneous with the Auvernier culture in western Switzerland, replaced the Horgen culture farther east. Originating in the north-east and scattered in several places through Europe, it invaded the Swiss Plateau and, like the earlier cultures, settled particularly round the lakes. It seems to have infiltrated Haute-Savoie, but did not penetrate the mountainous area, with the possible exception of the Grisons canton (Petrushügel, Cazis GR).

Plate 19

Fig. 16

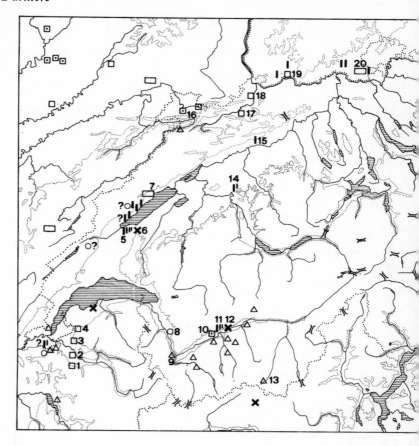

As in the Auvernier culture, the type of dwelling during the Corded-Ware period is the lake-dwelling – we will return to this later on. There are only a few examples of Corded-Ware burials in Switzerland. At Schöfflisdorf ZH, there is a cluster of over thirty round-barrows built over cremations. They were made of earth and stones laid alternately. Traces of post-holes were revealed, forming a rectangular plan of 5 × 3.3 m in one of the Zigiholz barrows at Sarmenstorf AG (as no implement was found it is impossible to affirm its links with Corded-Ware culture);

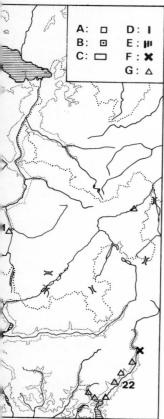

Fig. 18 Neolithic and later megaliths and rock-art. A, dolmen; B, dolmen with entrance or bored slab; C, passage-grave; D, menhir; E, group of menhirs; F,G, rock-engravings (F, Neolithic; G, later or undatable).

1–4, Haute-Savoie F (1, Pers-Jussy, destroyed; 2, Reignier; 3, Cranves-Sales, destroyed; 4, Saint-Cergues); 5, Yverdon VD; 6, Chavanne-le-Chêne VD, Vallon des Vaux; 7, Auvernier NE; 8, Bex VD (?); 9, Salvan VS; 10–11, Sion VS (10, Petit-Chasseur, engraved stelae); 12, Saint-Léonard VS; 13, Zermatt VS, Hübelwangen; 14, Bolligen BE; 15, Attiswil BE; 16, Courgenay BE, Pierre Percée; 17, Laufen BE; 18, Aesch BL; 19, Schwörstadt D; 20, Degernau D; 21, Sils-im-Domleschg GR, Carschenna; 22, Val Camonica I. Thin dotted line: 700 m altitude

it can be assumed that these were the remains of a wooden hut, a 'house of the dead'. In any case, apart from one occurrence in the Middle Neolithic cemetery at Lenzburg AG, the practice of cremation appears with the Late Neolithic. It seems only natural to think that this custom came from the north-east together with the culture as a whole.

As its name suggests, this culture is characterized by pottery with a typical decoration of cords, or imitation cords, applied on the clay when still soft. They are applied on vessels made of a rather fine clay: beakers

Plate 20, Fig. 19

63

with unpronounced profile and pots (called 'amphorae' by some) with a very marked girth. Along with the latter, there are pot-bellied containers with a very open neck made of a coarser clay and decorated with applied wavy bands. There are no handles, only perforated lugs. The bases are always flat. There are also wooden vessels, generally with a flat base.

The Corded-Ware culture is sometimes called the Battle-Axe culture. Certainly, one of its most specific elements is a well-formed perforated hammer-axe which is considered to be a weapon of war. There are other polished axes of a more usual type which were fixed to the haft by means of a casing; the most characteristic of these has a double-flanged butt. The flint tools and weapons as well as the bone and stag antler implements are not very different from those of the Auvernier culture. Among others, there are again the beautiful daggers made of imported flint. It has been shown clearly that they are imitations of copper weapons of similar shape, just as the bone pins (crutch-headed, wheel-headed, etc.) roughly imitate metal artifacts. However, only rarely do copper implements appear at certain Corded-Ware sites: flat axes and small daggers, handled awls, personal ornaments (small tubes and beads).

Though this culture did not last long, it has been possible to perceive variations which could be due to its evolution from a common background (the unitary horizon, 'Einheitshorizont', of C. Strahm). This could be the result of the arrival and rapid spread of newcomers who brought to south-east Switzerland a homogeneous culture which

Fig. 21

Fig. 20

Fig. 19 Late Neolithic; Corded-Ware culture; ceramics from Vinelz-Fénil BE (1–2), Zurich-Utoquai and Schöfflisdorf ZH (barrow). Max. ht. 16 cm

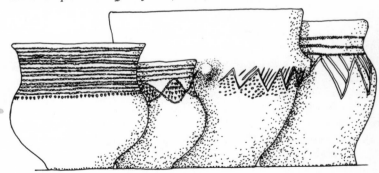

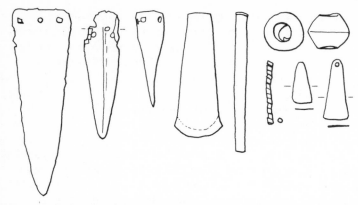

Fig. 20 Late Neolithic; Corded-Ware culture; Vinelz-Fénil BE. Left to right: copper implements (daggers, flat axe and chisel) and ornaments. Max. length c. 18 cm (but beads c. 3 cm long)

originated in the north-east. Thus, regional groups were formed differing from one another because of either their stage of evolution, or the arrival of new groups or the influence of indigenous or neighbouring cultures. A Sutz group (Sutz BE) has been distinguished, fairly close to the basic culture, and a late Zurich-Utoquai group.

The Schöfflisdorf round-barrows are rather different from those in the rest of Switzerland; they possibly derive from a German group and represent a very localized extension of it.

We shall discuss later a site of special interest, namely Petit-Chasseur at Sion, whose remains are attributable to the Late Neolithic. Here a dolmen burial of a distinctive type was found with wonderfully engraved anthropomorphic stelae.

Fig. 21 Late Neolithic; Vinelz-Fénil BE; flint dagger with wooden handle attached by a withe of clematis. Length c. 20 cm. Redrawn after C. Strahm, JBHM, 1961–62

THE LATEST NEOLITHIC

The Bell-Beaker culture Fifteen years ago, Switzerland was still not of particular interest for the study of this culture. Only a few typical implements, isolated or associated with assemblages of another culture (as for instance one sherd from the Schöfflisdorf round-barrow), showed the influence of this group. Since then, however, several discoveries have renewed the question by proving that the cultural current had penetrated

Fig. 16

and settled sporadically between both the Swiss Rhône and the Rhine. We said 'cultural current', but we could speak of 'immigrants'. Indeed, it is well known that the archers bearing the Bell-Beaker must have travelled swiftly through Europe in small groups; they would have passed through indigenous populations belonging to a great number of different cultures. They did not destroy them, but merely settled among them for long or short periods and borrowed from them various cultural elements, as for instance funerary rites and constructions. They have been compared to explorers, pioneers and gipsies. It is important to stress that the Bell-Beaker people were interested in metals, then a new discovery, mainly copper, gold and also silver. This explains their creation of well-established and distinctive centres in more than one region in Europe where copper sources are found, the most significant being those of southern Germany and the Iberian Peninsula.

It is, therefore, not surprising that these groups should have been discovered in Switzerland in an area where the existence of many copper and bronze implements during the Early Bronze Age suggests that copper ore was within reach: namely in the Valais canton. Excavations carried out since 1961 in Petit-Chasseur Street at Sion have brought to light the presence of a Bell-Beaker group who made use of the Late Neolithic dolmens and built other tombs imitating them, sometimes taking anthropomorphic stelae for certain slabs. This Petit-Chasseur complex has many consequences for the understanding of both Swiss and Alpine prehistory from 3000 to 1500 BC and will be dealt with separately. It can be said now that the Bell-Beaker pottery found here belongs to two different stages, corresponding to migrations from opposite geographical areas: from the Rhine, Bavarian and Bohemian areas to the north, and from the Mediterranean region to the south-west. Unfortunately the copper implements were removed later when the tombs were plundered but traces of them indicate their presence. There are also two ornaments: one is in gold (a small ring belonging to the Unětice-Aunjetitz culture), the other in silver (an ear-ornament also of Eastern European origin). It is of interest to see migrating Bell-Beaker peoples, coming from varied backgrounds, settle in the upper valley of the Rhône not far from the Alpine passes.

The other centre where Bell-Beaker peoples settled is the Rhine elbow, around Basle. Unfortunately we know little of the circumstances of the discovery (generally in tombs) of the artifacts which testify to their presence. This is true not only for Switzerland – Allschwil and Riehen BS, Muttenz BL – but also for Saint-Louis in France, and Kirchen and Efringen in Germany.

The site of Petit-Chasseur at Sion VS   This site is located at the western entrance to the capital of the Valais canton, at the foot of a steep mountain slope which the Rhône in spate does not often reach but where the neighbouring torrent, the Sionne, might carry enormous masses of earth and stones which have fortunately covered and protected the prehistoric remains. Here there is an archaeological sequence from the Middle Neolithic (*c.* 3500 B C) up to the end of the Early Bronze Age (1500 B C), as well as Celtic burials from the very beginning of the Roman occupation.

We may mention in passing the Middle Neolithic level which has already been touched on briefly and which is the first sign of the colonization of Valais. The foundations of dwellings, with pits (silos, kilns, etc.), probably belong to the Saint-Léonard group and are dated by C14 to between 3500 and 2800 B C. Several cist-burials discovered in this level link this type of burial with the Cortaillod-Chassey-Lagozza culture. The menhir alignments some distance away could possibly belong to that same culture.

After a few centuries of desertion, with a break (proved by a hearth with an arrowhead) *c.* 2300 B C, the site was reoccupied by Late Neolithic people *c.* 2200 B C. They erected a large dolmen tomb (M VI) with an opening in one angle of the eastern wall sealed with a small removable slab. This dolmen was built on a base of a form hitherto unknown: it is a long isosceles triangle with a 6 m base and a present height of 16 m (originally 16.5 – 17 m), surrounded by a small dry-stone wall made of uniformly cut stones and filled with irregular slabs. We have good reason to suppose that several large anthropomorphic stelae   Plate 21, *Fig. 22* stood in front of the base of the monument. There are no longer any standing because they were re-used later as building materials for cists and dolmens.

Following the 1973 excavations the number of stelae recovered (often very fragmentary) rose to twenty-six. These works of art are made on shiny schist slabs of variable thickness (a rock found on the neighbouring slope), carefully cut to obtain a rectangle, the body topped

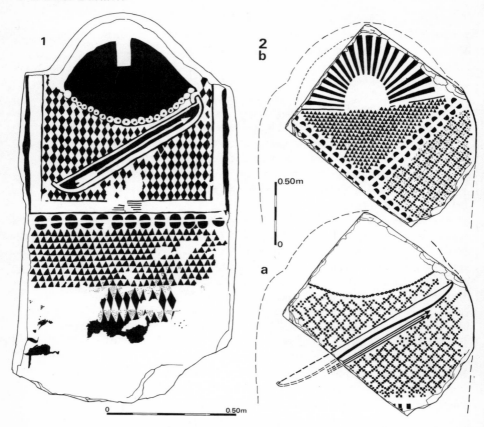

Fig. 22 Late Neolithic in the Alps; Sion VS, Petit-Chasseur; anthropomorphic stelae (the engravings are in black). 1, one of the stelae of the external cist of dolmen M XI (see plate 24); 2, dolmen M I, northern stele: hypothetical reconstruction of the two stages of engraving

by a semicircle to suggest the head. As a rule, the surface of the body is dotted to depict the arms folded at right-angles, with the stretched-out fingers of both hands nearly touching. Only on two of the stelae can the face be seen, roughly indicated by a 'T' representing the eyebrows and the nose, as on certain engravings in the French subterranean chambers of the S.O.M. culture. Clothing is generally represented by an ingenious combination of squares, lozenges, herring-bone patterns and dots, along with a neck-collar (or scarf) of several rows and a belt which emphasizes the forearms – a shoulder-belt is more rarely found. Under this belt there is sometimes a kind of apron which suggests the sporran of a Scottish kilt. Some of the stelae also have under the belt a dagger with a triangular blade and central rib and a large pommelled haft.

The dating of these stelae has been debated for a long time. Here we follow A. Gallay's hypothesis: he stresses the similarity of the triangular-bladed dagger to those found in northern Italy (Gaudo culture, dated *c.* 2300 BC). This date is not incompatible with the presence on the first stele found of a large copper pectoral ornament suggesting a double spiral. This motif is known in the cultures of the Central European Chalcolithic (Hungary, Slovakia, Austria) and Eastern Europe (Poland) at the end of the fourth millennium BC. This is much earlier than the suggested date, but this can be explained by the survival of an ancient form in a work of art with definite religious significance (representation of a divinity or ancestor).

What remains of the funerary goods left by the builders of dolmen M VI belongs unquestionably to the Late Neolithic: daggers made of Grand-Pressigny flint, stone spindle-whorls, etc. It is difficult to tell exactly to which culture of this period one should assign the building, stelae and implements. They might be the work of a local Alpine group related to the Auvernier culture, with possible connections with northern Italy. There is a dolmen and anthropomorphic stelae at Saint-Martin-de-Corléans near Aosta, directly beneath the Alps crossing the Great Saint-Bernard pass.

Fig. 23

When the first Bell-Beaker people arrived, did they build their tombs by breaking and re-using the stelae which had fallen into disuse and had lost any meaning? The question seems complex and it is not impossible that both the making and destruction of the stelae continued for several centuries. These Bell-Beaker people used implements and made a plain patterned pottery which suggests a Central European and Rhine origin, with some vessels from the southern valley of the Rhône. They robbed tomb M VI and interred their own dead in it, along with their ornaments of bone, boars' teeth, copper (these have disappeared), silver and gold.

Plate 22, *Fig. 24*

Plates 24, 25

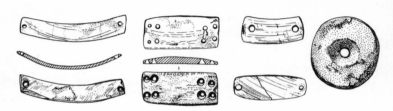

Fig. 23 Late Neolithic in the Alps; Sion VS, Petit-Chasseur; sample of the grave-goods (flint dagger, 'thumb-guards' and spindle-whorl) from the period of the first dolmen (M VI). Length of dagger c. 5.7 cm

It can be assumed that these newcomers imitated what they saw and built the other smaller barrows (M I, M XI) and cists, using the anthropomorphic stelae as common building material.

Nearly all these tombs were robbed at the beginning of the Early Bronze Age (c. 1950 BC) by men who placed vessels in or beside some of them. Finally, towards the end of this period (c. 1500 BC) a house was built, related to the ancient burials; new tombs were established following a much simpler pattern but with rich gifts of ornaments and bronze weapons.

The conclusions based on the finds at Petit-Chasseur are obviously of great interest: the presence of megalithic monuments in the heart of the Alpine zone; the religious and artistic expressions of the Late Neolithic period related to the better-known examples on the Italian slopes of the Alps; the appearance of the Bell-Beaker people and, finally, elements linked to the introduction of copper as early as the Neolithic.

CONCLUSIONS

Considering the whole of the Swiss Neolithic, the impression emerges of a rapid and intense colonization. It is true that the first farmers were attracted by the Plateau and the lower slopes of the Jura, but they did not take long to reach the Alps. In the Middle Neolithic they were settled in the valley leading to the Great Saint-Bernard pass at Sembrancher VS, about 700 m high, and also in the valley of Conches, upstream from Brig, as far as Bitsch VS at the same altitude; this is on the way to the Furka pass.

The Late Neolithic site of Petrushügel at Cazis GR and the similar sites of Sion and in the Italian valley of Aosta have already been

Fig. 24 Late Neolithic in the Alps; Bell-Beaker culture; Sion VS, Petit-Chasseur; beakers of various types (partly reconstructed). Max. ht. c. 16 cm

mentioned. Further evidence is afforded by a large axe with a pointed butt of Atlantic type which was found above Zermatt, at an altitude of 2400 m, on the way to the Théodule pass. Several tanged arrowheads found in the Alps indicate that hunters had passed by. During the Late Neolithic, Bell-Beaker groups also settled at Sion VS. Penetration of the folded Jura zone was a slower process. The settlers did not have to cross this range which was shorter and narrower than the Alps; since it was less open, most preferred to pass round it. In any case, there is no Neolithic site here whereas the shores of lakes Neuchâtel and Bienne, located at the south-east foot of the Jura, indicate a dense population; the same applies to the other side of the range in Franche-Comté.

TRANSALPINE SWITZERLAND

The question is still discussed of the Neolithization of the Tessin and the nearby Grisons valleys (Mesolcina and Val Calanca) which belong to the Po basin and are separated by high ridges from the basins of the Rhône and the Rhine. The presence of a few isolated finds – arrowheads and polished axes – give only unreliable indications. It can be assumed that this territory was occupied occasionally as far as some of the valleys (for instance Olivone, Val Blenio, at about 1000 m). No site or burial of the Neolithic period is yet known, with the possible exception of Coldrerio. Moreover, we know almost nothing about the conditions of discovery of the flint implements.

The absence of evidence for the colonization of the Tessin by the first agriculturists is even more incomprehensible owing to the proximity of the rich centres of the north Italian Lagozza culture. Coldrerio is about 20 km from the sites of lake Varèse, with no natural barrier separating them. As far as our present knowledge goes, it can be said that Transalpine relations existed between the Valais and northern Italy, though this was not the case farther east: the valleys of the central and eastern Alps in Switzerland were not even tentatively penetrated from the south. Recent discoveries in Trentin and especially in the valley of the upper Adige have revealed Mesolithic and Neolithic sites showing that a well-conducted excavation can immediately necessitate the revision of notions which hitherto have been taken for granted. Let us hope that this will be the case in the Tessin.

CHAPTER IV

The Problem of the Lake-dwellings

While dealing with Neolithic cultures lake- and moor-dwellings have been mentioned on several occasions and they will be considered again when dealing with the Bronze Age. Since the problem of this type of dwelling has given rise to considerable discussion, it will be useful here to summarize the different elements involved as well as the present interpretation of structures observed underwater and those under the lake banks and peat.

The phenomena we are concerned with are not specifically Swiss; lake-dwellings are also found on both sides of the Alps, in French, Italian, German, Austrian and Yugoslavian territories and even farther afield. But the lakes and peat-bogs of Switzerland have provided extensive remains from many sites which have been known for a long time.

A short historical account will help us understand how the idea of pile-dwellings captured the imagination of scholars and public alike, and how it developed under sometimes excessive criticism which did nevertheless provoke reconsideration of previously held views. During the winter of 1853–54 the discovery of a lake-dwelling at Obermeilen ZH was accepted as a scientific fact. A few months later, Ferdinand Keller reported this discovery as well as that of other sites uncovered shortly after the first. Indeed, besides giving a detailed description of the structures and implements, this Zurich archaeologist also attempted to reconstruct a lake-dwelling. He concluded (in the introduction to the English translation of his first surveys in 1866) 'that from a series of discoveries the fact is made manifest, that in the very earliest times groups of families, or probably whole tribes, subsisting by hunting and fishing, with some knowledge of agriculture, lived on the borders of the Swiss lakes, in huts built not on dry ground, but on a series of piles in the shallows near the shores'.

In order to illustrate this point of view, he published in his first account (1854) a drawing of a lake-dwelling explaining that his model was the illustrated description given by Dumont d'Urville of the village of Dorei in New Guinea. The similarities between one of d'Urville's engravings and F. Keller's drawing is striking.

To make his reconstruction, Keller combined two methods. Firstly, with the archaeological techniques perfected in the mid-nineteenth century he was able to confirm the existence of piles underwater which had been fixed in a specific order, surrounded by a layer of organic matter containing many artifacts. Secondly, he used the comparative ethnographic method, showing the actual existence in distant countries of villages built on piles above the water. During the following years, this comparative research led to the recognition of similar settlements on water in several continents as well as in antiquity.

The picture thus established and then adapted slightly by F. Keller was a complete success and remained the only accepted representation for nearly a century. It was (and sometimes still is) printed not only in school history books but also in paintings and models on view in museums. It is significant to note that when, during the twentieth century, protests were raised against such an interpretation, they gave rise not only to scientific discussion but also to almost emotional reactions among the general public; it was as though questioning the popular image was an attack on the national heritage.

As early as 1923, however, Paul Vouga came to the conclusion that, on the basis of his excavation with improved techniques of the shoreline sites at lake Neuchâtel, these dwellings were not built on the lake but on the part of the shore which was periodically flooded. Consequently, the dwellings would have been held up by short piles. The theory, however, received no immediate support.

Not long after new criticisms were raised against F. Keller's classical theory. The first protests came from Hans Reinerth, a German archaeologist known for his excavations at several sites in southern Germany and for his book on the Neolithic of Switzerland (1926). From his own observations he was led to a conclusion rather similar to P. Vouga's: the lake- and moor-dwellings were not built on the water 'but on the shore, partly on the meadows of sedge and moss and partly on the dry non-marshy ground'. Some of the dwellings were directly on the ground, others were above it, supported by very short piles. The Swiss archaeologists reacted strongly against this statement. The most interesting arguments were expressed by the naturalists who, on the strength of conclusions drawn from the study of plant remains and molluscs, refused to accept the new interpretation. We will discuss this point later on.

After the Second World War another German archaeologist and engineer, Otto Paret, once again vigorously attacked the classical view of the lake-dwellings. At first his arguments were technical. Without going into detail we will quote some of them: supposing that the piles did go through several metres of water, they would not have been numerous enough to bear the weight of a platform and timber huts with clay hearths and equipment, particularly if one considers the pressure exerted by the wind, waves, snow and ice. The fragile nature of the frames as they were then imagined (with bindings made of vegetable fibres), made the idea even more impossible. Moreover, the pole-pile arrangements attached by forks or notches or mortise joints are known only from a few examples. The floors, coated with clay, which were found at several sites are conceivable only if laid directly on the ground – if they had been placed as a platform on piles they would have become unstable and the clay would have cracked immediately. If the floors had been laid on damp ground they would have been more stable and have offered some protection. Fences made of close-set posts had frequently been interpreted as break-waters when facing out into the lake, and as defence walls when they were erected between the site and solid land. Paret showed that the break-water could not have resisted for long decay and the movement of the water, and that the defensive barriers would have been too fragile to withstand quick destruction. If we consider the nature and diameter of the posts it seems likely that these fences were the remains of enclosures around the village which were frequently replaced (this explains the disorder of the plans, as new posts were added without removing the bases of the old ones).

Paret's sometimes over-dogmatic theories provoked strong criticism in which the press was involved, but the main outcome of his arguments was to draw the attention of archaeologists excavating lake- and moor-dwellings to the necessity of careful scrutiny in order to verify or invalidate Paret's important statements. In the course of detailed excavations some of them, such as E. Vogt, had already become aware of facts which led them to modify their opinions on the subject. When the

Swiss Society of Prehistory celebrated the centenary of the discovery of Obermeilen by publishing a collective work (*Das Pfahlbauproblem*, 1955), Vogt contributed an important paper of 100 pages in which he supported Paret's ideas, introducing new arguments based partly on his own observations. He concluded that it was now up to the supporters of the classical theory (i.e. pile-dwellings above the water) to justify their position; this was addressed mainly to the naturalists.

Since 1955 archaeologists in several parts of Switzerland have excavated various types of lake- and moor-dwellings in different environments (near small and large lakes, streams, etc.) and have gained a clearer understanding, with the help of naturalists, of the location and character of the settlements. These investigations have, on the whole, led to the conclusion that dwellings were erected on the shore, though some points still need clarification.

We have already referred to the naturalists' opposition to the 'land' interpretation of lake-dwellings and will briefly return to it as their arguments are valuable. A. Jayet, a geologist, thought that the prehistoric sediments could be explained only if the ground into which man had driven the piles had been under water (not very deep). The analysis of molluscs found in the lake-dwellings confirmed this opinion: J. Favre had demonstrated as early as 1928 that the molluscs all belonged to aquatic species. From an examination of the plant remains the botanists, including W. Ludi in 1955, deduced that the climate during the Bronze Age would not have allowed a lowering of the lake-levels sufficient to dry up the sites of the lake-dwellings.

It is impossible to discuss these arguments here in detail, but it would seem feasible to adapt them to the new theory, once it is assumed that the ground supporting the dwellings was water-logged. So far as the molluscs are concerned, it is not surprising that the water covering the abandoned site allowed these aquatic species to settle in the loose organic layers deposited by man; while the calcareous shells of the land molluscs which might have lived on the site could have been destroyed either by trampling or by the action of acids. The most difficult question to resolve is the problem of the depth of several Bronze Age sites in connection with the possible drainage of the lakes when the water-level drops just below the bench-mark of the lowest site.

To conclude, in most cases the lake- and moor-dwellings of the

Neolithic and Bronze Age were not built over the water but on the shore which had been recently uncovered as a result of a fall in the water-level. Since the ground was very damp protection was needed; this was secured – very unsatisfactorily – by a bed of oak bark laid on the earth, or interlaced branches or floors made of closely-set poles that were partly or entirely covered with a coat of clay. The vertical beams of the frame had to be sunk rather deeply into the damp ground and replaced quite often (due to their rotting above ground). This frequent renewal explains the confusion in site plans when all the piles have been drawn; in fact, it is generally difficult to trace house plans without conjecturing the clay floors and sometimes the fallen walls. In these dwellings, there were one or more hearths, often made of a clay slab. This gradually sank when it was put directly on the earth; in such a case a new coat of clay was applied which gave, in section, a lenticular form with alternating layers of clay and ashes.

Between the dwellings and firm ground corduroy roads were built, sometimes secured by piles, which explains why they might at first have been interpreted as foot-bridges. Finally the dwelling or group of dwellings was partly or entirely surrounded by a barrier or fence to keep cattle in. Stables and manure have been found.

Plate 23

It is clear that the proposed picture is less romantic and less original than the one put forward by F. Keller. It has the advantage of eliminating the question: why build on the water? Certainly there is still the question of why the settlements were constructed on such damp ground when firmer land lay only a few metres away. The answer may depend on the vegetational conditions of the time: the primary deciduous forest covered most of Switzerland during the Neolithic period. The Neolithic and Bronze Age farmers needed fields to grow corn, barley and millet. Since such fields could not be located on the shoreline where there was no arable land they had to use clearings, or create them by burning. They would therefore have built their dwellings in the spaces between the forest and the water.

Theoretically the existence of pile-dwellings cannot yet be ruled out; but these buildings at the water's edge, constructed of a small platform fixed to short piles in shallow water, might only have been isolated cases. This is close to the views of H. Reinerth and P. Vouga but it still has to be proved.

The Problem of the Lake-dwellings

As stated earlier, use of the ethnographic comparative method to demonstrate that lake-dwellings were built over the water is not justified. The presence of pile-dwellings in south-east Asia, Oceania and South America only indicates that similar buildings might have existed in prehistoric Europe, but climate and its implications still have to be considered. Only careful scrutiny of a meticulous excavation could provide the necessary determining factors.

CHAPTER V

The Early Bronze Age

The division between the end of the Neolithic and the first phase of the Bronze Age is more arbitrary than any other. In Switzerland, as elsewhere in Europe, the first metal appeared among groups which belong unquestionably to the Neolithic by their cultural context. To overcome this difficulty, expressions uniting the two technological notions of 'stone' and 'metal' (copper, bronze) are used: Eneolithic, Copper Age, or Chalcolithic. Such terms do not seem necessary in Switzerland because when metal appeared it was at first part of a slow penetration of copper implements which do not characterize the cultures in which they were found. They indicate that the first metallurgy was already established elsewhere when Neolithic Switzerland appeared to be 'a country in the process of development'. This is seen in the scarcity of tools and ornaments recovered at the Middle Neolithic sites (Cortaillod and Pfyn cultures) and Late Neolithic sites (Horgen and Corded-Ware cultures). In the latter, the influence of more developed neighbouring countries is also shown by bone objects (various pins) and flint implements (daggers) which imitate similar copper objects.

There may have been a more or less peaceful coexistence between some of the Late Neolithic populations and the first groups bearing the Early Bronze Age culture. This overlap is attested not only by the sites and finds belonging to these two stages. It is as if populations of different cultural traditions had simultaneously occupied distinct zones. This is clear enough for western Switzerland and neighbouring France. When the Corded-Ware culture (centred on the lakes of Neuchâtel, Bienne and Morat and more generally on the Plateau) and the Bell-Beaker groups were at their highest density in the Saône valley and on the Rhine, the people of the Early Bronze Age formed an Alpine and Rhône-Alpine province. This means that the Neolithic cultures in question lasted long enough to witness the introduction of the first metallurgy. It is

Figs. 16, 25

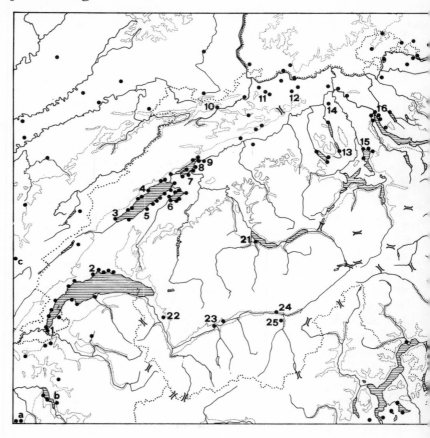

only during the last phase (4) of the Early Bronze Age that the new culture exists alone.

In fact, we do not know how metallurgy and bronze penetrated into Switzerland. It is only logical to think that the first metal objects found on Neolithic sites had been imported from reasonably far-off production centres. East-Central Europe certainly played a leading part, which was to continue in the development of the Unetice (Aunjetitz) culture in central Germany and Bohemia. But it has already been asked with

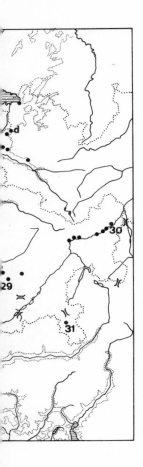

Fig. 25 Bronze Age settlements. 1, *Geneva;* 2, *Morges VD;* 3, *Grandson VD, Corcelettes;* 4, *Auvernier NE;* 5, *Estavayer-le-Lac FR;* 6, *Avenches VD, Eau Noire;* 7, *Lüscherz-Locras BE;* 8, *Mörigen BE;* 9, *Nidau and Port BE;* 10, *Courroux BE;* 11, *Sissach BL;* 12, *Wittnau BL, Wittnauer Horn;* 13, *Baldegg LU;* 14, *Möriken AG, Kestenberg;* 15, *Zug-Sumpf ZG;* 16, *Zurich;* 17, *Kreuzlingen TG;* 18, *Arbon TG, Bleiche;* 19, *Oberriet SG, Montlingerberg;* 20, *Mels SG;* 21, *Spiez BE, Burg;* 22, *Ollon VD, Saint-Triphon;* 23, *Sion VS;* 24, *Raron-Rarogne VS;* 25, *Zeneggen VS, Kastels;* 26, *Fellers GR, Muota;* 27, *Lumbrein GB, Crestaulta;* 28, *Cazis GR, Cresta;* 29, *Savognin GR, Patnal;* 30, *Ramosch GR, Mottata;* 31, *Poschiavo GR, Pedenal.*
Outside Switzerland: a, *lake of Bourget F;* b, *lake of Annecy F;* c, *lake of Chalain F;* d, *Koblach AU;* e, *Como I.*
Thin dotted line: 700 m altitude

regard to the arrival of the Bell-Beaker people in Valais whether they were attracted by the presence of copper-ore deposits in this region of the Alps. It will be discussed later. This phenomenon could have happened again and become more marked during the Bronze Age, considering the rapid rise of this culture in the Alpine zone. But if metal were found there, it is certain that the rest of the country had none. This scarcity of copper in Switzerland explains the influence exerted on indigenous populations by the foreign metallurgical centres.

The immigration of foreign groups bearing the new technique has not been mentioned. Without excluding such relatively restricted migratory movements it seems more likely that only specialists and metal-workers brought from outside Switzerland the technological knowledge and finished implements. They sold the implements and, in some cases, settled among the tribes of Neolithic tradition who were interested in their production and benefited from it. It is certainly hypothetical but it explains the diversification observed among human groups in Switzerland. This diversification may result from the transplanting of copper and bronze techniques to cultures of different Neolithic origins and in various geographical areas.

Study of metal-working techniques during the Early Bronze Age has therefore made it possible to distinguish two types of implement whose distributions, both in space and time, show significant differences. On the one hand, there are the groups that obtained these artifacts by moulding (as in the Únětice culture and its derivatives) and, on the other hand, there are those that worked by hammering the metal to give a sheet-bronze. These latter groups (Kisapostag in Hungary, Straubing in Bavaria and the Rhône culture in Switzerland) have sometimes been called the 'sheet-bronze group' (*Blechkreis*). This single technological criterion should not, of course, be considered too important but it certainly represents an interesting aspect of the diversification in question.

CHRONOLOGY OF THE EARLY BRONZE AGE

The remarks above may serve as an introduction to what is still called the Early Bronze Age, bearing in mind that when it began it coexisted with the last few hundred years of the Late Neolithic. The chronology of this period has been widely discussed and charts are numerous but vary according to typological criteria and to the area in question. Most archaeologists still consider Reinecke's original classification (1902) to be definitive. Early Bronze could correspond with his A and B periods (each sub-divided into 1 and 2). This quadripartite division is usually kept but with different numbering. Sangmeister (1966), then A. and G. Gallay (1968) proposed a simpler distinction of phases 1 to 4. These are not merely technical points, because in fact phase 4 is different from the other three phases and represents the later part of the Early Bronze Age. It is possible to consider phases 1 and 3 as the period of coexistence with the Corded-Ware culture.

In the opinion of some authors, the technological difference referred to above (moulded bronze, hammered sheet-bronze) could correspond to a chronological distribution. The first manifestations of the Early Bronze Age would be those generally under the name of the 'Rhône culture' (or Valais culture; in German: *Rhonekultur* or *Walliser kultur*).

THE CONQUEST OF THE ALPS

The name 'Rhône culture' takes into account the great density and wealth of the Valais and of the part of the Vaud canton located on the eastern slope of the Rhône valley, upstream from lake Geneva. But this

Fig. 26 Early Bronze Age in the Alps; Rhône valley; copper and bronze objects of the beginning of the period (Bronze A or I). Left to right, top to bottom: torque (Aigle VD); large axe (Sion VS); trefoiled and oval-headed pins (Conthey VS); disc-headed pin and crescent-like pendant (Ayent VS); dagger blade (Ollon VD); engraved axe (Martigny VS); rolled-out armband (Villeneuve VD). Length of axe c. 35 cm

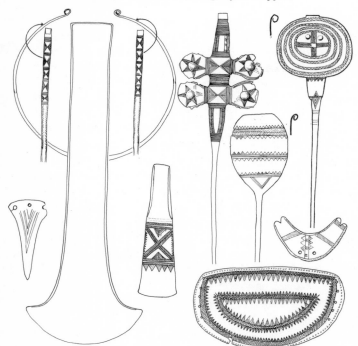

should not hide the fact that the culture is known outside this particular area. It existed in Gruyère FR, around Thoune BE and farther east in the upper basin of the Rhine. The mountainous setting of this cultural complex is evident and is even clearer, broadly speaking, when we see that the Swiss Rhône culture is linked to a vast European ensemble which stretches from the French Rhône valley to Austria through the Italian and Swiss Alps. It is true that farther east the west Hungarian province is not mountainous, but it is one of the original centres of the complex as are other secondary isolated centres located farther north.

We know that the Neolithic people were not afraid to penetrate into the Alpine regions, sometimes climbing quite high, and that they went through several passes. But, though they settled in the great valleys (Rhône, Rhine), they hardly colonized the higher regions. At the beginning of the Bronze Age, however, men took an increasing interest in these regions. They must have been motivated, particularly in the Valais, by the search for copper sources possibly existing in some of the high valleys (copper pyrites in Les Vals d'Hérens and Anniviers). But it is probable that at the same time they discovered the advantages of the mountain meadows for their herds and that a real pastoral colonization would then have taken place. The valleys leading to the passes certainly have a greater density of objects and show that the Rhône group was not inward-looking, but kept contacts with its neighbours and even sought contacts with more distant groups.

Material wealth   The metal implements and ornaments of this group are well known from many objects, unfortunately often isolated finds made when the tombs had been destroyed. A thorough typological compara-tive analysis of all these objects has been necessary to establish their chronological and geographical classification.

Fig. 26

The most important types of metal objects are of sheet-bronze made by hammering. This is evidently not the case for the axes which could have been imported from the Plateau (axe of Neyruz type). The very simple triangular dagger blade rapidly evolved into the beautiful Rhône dagger, decorated and fixed into a heavy metal handle made by the moulding technique. Metal ornaments are varied, especially the pins (bulb-headed, trefoil – simple or double – crook-headed and lozenge-shaped). In addition, there is the strong wired torque terminating in eyelets, the diadem (not so frequent), a long strip of engraved sheet-metal, the bow-shaped pendant and the armlet, both of engraved sheet-metal. Sheet-metal tubes were grouped together to form bracelets and necklaces. There are also non-metal ornaments such as V-perforated conical buttons, biconical bone beads and Mediterranean *Columbella rustica* shells.

This description applies in particular to the first three phases of the Early Bronze Age. The fourth is partly a continuation of the earlier phases (daggers, certain pins), though it is distinguished by the disappearance of several types (torques, diadems, trefoil pins) and by the appearance of the disc-headed pin with engraved and chased decoration. The most spectacular specimen (the only one outside the Valais) comes from Muota (Fellers GR) and is 0.85 m long. There also appear new axe shapes (spatula-axes or palstaves, spatula-chisel-axes, etc.) which show great mastery of bronze metalwork. That this industry improved is shown by the replacement of the hammering technique by casting. The influence of the Plateau province is reflected in all the finished goods and imported new ideas.

Plate 26

E. Vogt found a genetic connection between the types of bronze objects found in the Rhône culture and the two fairly distant provinces with the names of two type sites: Straubing in Bavaria and Kisapostag in Hungary. The Swiss Alpine group and the closely related communities in the French Rhône, northern Italy and Austria would have resulted from the imposition of technological methods brought from these regions on the Late Neolithic and the Bell-Beaker cultures.

Little is known of the pottery of this group, especially during its first stages. It seems to have lost the fine and highly decorative technique which characterizes the end of the Neolithic. Indeed, the pottery consists of thick-walled jars of a rather soft ware with a fairly coarse temper and decorated with low relief cords (mainly horizontal), sometimes bearing finger impressions. Towards the end of this period, however, another pottery type appears made of finer ware, with thinner walls and handles.

Plate 27

Dwellings are beginning to be better known, thanks to systematic excavations in several areas. In the Valais canton at Petit-Chasseur, Sion, a few post-holes provided evidence of a wooden house. There are other signs of human settlement on the rocky hills overlooking the Rhône valley, at Collombey-Muraz (Barmaz I) and Saint-Léonard.

It is in the Grisons canton that one can best observe how these Early Bronze Age people of the Alpine valleys settled the land. Taking

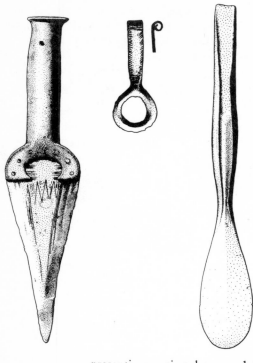

Fig. 27   Early Bronze Age in the Alps; Sion VS, Petit-Chasseur; bronze-hilted dagger, pendant and spoon-axe, found in graves of the end of the period. Length of dagger c. 20 cm

precautions against the natural elements (avalanche, flood) and possible enemies they chose, as in the Valais, rocky ridges emerging from the mountain slopes and overlooking the valley bottom. On these they built small houses either entirely of wood (Muota-Fellers GR) or with light stone foundations, as in the rocky hill site of Cresta at Cazis GR where houses 3–4 m × 4–5 m in size, with hearths made of small slabs, succeeded one another for several levels.

Burials of the Early Bronze Age people are well known. The greater part of the archaeological material belonging to this period in the Alpine valleys comes from burials. The same applies in the Valais to the small Barmaz I cemetery (Collombey-Muraz) which followed the Middle Neolithic tombs. The bodies had been buried under the earth in an extended position on their backs, sometimes surrounded by a few rocks. It seems that nothing marked the tomb, as there is evidence of previously

Plate 28

Plate 29

buried skeletons which had been disturbed and partly removed when a second pit was dug. The grave-goods, poor at Barmaz I, were sometimes very rich elsewhere, as is seen from the remarkable examples of Le Lessus (Ollon VD) on the other side of the Rhône valley, as well as at Petit-Chasseur, Sion VS. At these sites two burials contained several objects of very good quality, including a spatula-axe, placed under the head in both cases. All these tombs belong to the end of the Early Bronze Age. As for the earlier period the Petit-Chasseur dolmen (M XI), excavated in 1973, may be noted. It had been built by the Bell-Beaker people and was re-used for several later burials.

Fig. 27

In the Grisons at Donath in the upper valley of the Rhine (Hinterrhein), one tomb indicates a special rite: two bodies were buried together in an inverted position, the head of one body level with the other's feet. This practice has been observed west of the Plateau at Saint-Martin FR near Oron VD.

THE EARLY BRONZE AGE ON THE PLATEAU AND JURA

It is in the Plateau and Jura regions that one can observe best the coexistence of the last stages of the Neolithic culture (principally the Corded-Ware culture) with the beginning of the Bronze Age. It is relevant to note that the most important sites with evidence of the Bronze Age are lake-dwellings, showing the persistence of a tradition all the more alive since it results from an immediately preceding period.

In these sites we have better-balanced samples of the material culture than in the burials which provide the majority of objects of the Rhône group. The pottery is well understood. It is generally of good quality with a fine polished slip. The most typical shape is the low handled cup (called the Les Roseaux cup after a Morges lake-dwelling). But the forms are rather diversified, with cups, plates, bowls and jugs. The decoration of geometric motifs is simple (lines, triangles, etc.). One pattern of dots bordered by a wavy line recalls a similar theme on some corded vessels. There is also coarser pottery, including storage-jars decorated with finger-impressed cords.

Fig. 28

Bronze weapons and tools should be particularly noted as their variations may have a regional, probably ethnic, and chronological significance as far as they reflect changing fashions. The axe is

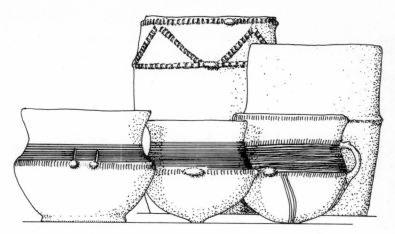

Fig. 28 Early Bronze Age; Morges VD, lake-dwelling of Les Roseaux; pottery (partly reconstructed). Ht. c. 10.5–11 cm (rear c. 36–42 cm)

characteristic in this respect. There is a series of well-defined types, all belonging to the primitive class of flanged axes which follows the simplest form of the flat axe. Among these flanged axes two different types may first be mentioned whose distribution is significant: the Salez axe (from a site in Rhine SG) and the Neyruz axe (from a site in Gruyère FR). While the former, apart from a few rare exceptions, is localized in north-east Switzerland, the Neyruz axe is restricted to the western half of the Plateau and the Jura, and to a lesser extent in the Valais. The dagger appears frequently, including the type with a metal hilt which probably came from the Rhône-Alpine region; similar daggers from the Plateau had hilts made of perishable material such as wood, and the blade is often decorated with V-shaped grooves. This dagger is characteristic of the Plateau at the end of the Early Bronze Age, though some examples were found in the Valais almost as far away as Sion. In addition to these weapons there are socketed lance-heads, tanged arrowheads together with simple tools: double-pointed awls, chisels, perforated needles and fish-hooks.

Metal ornaments are characteristic of this group and are numerous and varied, though they do not attain the richness of the Rhône-Alpine jewellery. Pins are again the most varied: vase-headed pins, heads with oblique perforation, knot-headed and spiral-headed pins (among them the so-called Horkheim pin), etc. There are open-ended bracelets, hair ornaments (spiral rings) and various pendants.

The culture of the Plateau and the surroundings of the Jura is linked to a greater complex, as is the Alps culture which penetrated the great valleys. It is also connected with Central Europe (Únětice-Aunjetitz culture) as well as with northern Italy, Franche-Comté and southern France. There are even indications of contact with more distant centres, for instance the fine long bronze flanged-axe from Renzenbühl (Thoune BE) which has a copper band inlaid with small gold plugs fixed on either face. This axe recalls Mycenaean objects, considered to have penetrated as far as Wessex, and its contemporaneity with the Wessex culture poses a question. This raises a chronological problem but the evidence will not be discussed here.

Plate 30

Domestic buildings We have already mentioned the lake-dwellings of the Swiss Early Bronze Age which carry on the Neolithic farmers' tradition of colonizing the sterile lake shores in order to cultivate the clearings. Over fifteen of these settlements are known but only two have been properly excavated: Bleiche (Arbon TG) on lake Constance and Baldegg (Hochdorf LU) on lake Baldegg. They reveal an architectural system following the Neolithic tradition but one which is still evolving. In this respect the Baldegg settlement is significant. Here, the Early Bronze Age site exactly covers the Late Neolithic settlement (Corded-Ware); both sites are surrounded by fences in the shape of an irregular arc of a circle, *c.* 54 m long, on the landward side with a hollow in it corresponding to the gate. The building of the houses was carefully executed. Plano-convex wooden blocks with central holes into which posts could be fixed were systematically used as bases; this prevented the posts from sinking into the very soft ground. This arrangement is seen again during the Late Bronze Age. It is, however, restricted to central and north-eastern Switzerland; the shores of the western lakes might have been firm enough to make the use of such structures unnecessary. At Baldegg it was possible to note a few methods of fixing horizontal beams to posts by means of mortise-and-tenon joints with pine branches lashed round several times. As in the Neolithic sites it is difficult to trace the layout of the houses from the agglomeration of piles. E. Vogt, working at Bleiche (Arbon TG) from K. Keller-Tarmuzzer's detailed plans, proposed layouts of 3 × 4 m to 4 × 8 m.

In addition to lake-dwellings, the Early Bronze Age peoples also carried on the tradition of occupying the higher regions already noted in the area of the Rhône-Alpine group (although to a lesser extent), as for instance on Bürglen (Untersiggenthal AG), overlooking the confluence between the Limmat and the Aar, and just across the border in the Rhine valley at Kadel (Koblach, Vorarlberg AU).

Burials Our knowledge of funerary rites on the Plateau is more fragmentary because many burials have been destroyed, leaving only tomb furniture which is, however, often rich. This is the case for the finds at Bois-de-Vaux and at La Bourdonnette (Lausanne VD), for example, although it is not certain whether they come from tombs or accompanied the child burial found in the earth (but close to a vertical slab) at Plant de Rives (Auvernier NE), very near the Neolithic dolmen tomb. It could be that observations made during the excavations are incomplete. We have already mentioned a tomb near Oron VD surrounded by stones in which two individuals had been buried head to toe along with bronze implements. It would have been of great interest to establish the sex of these two bodies and the orientation of the tomb. It can be concluded from the few available statements that there were hardly any variations in the funerary rites, in which inhumation predominates, with the body placed on its back and with a deposit of weapons and ornaments. Pottery, however, is virtually absent. The double inhumation of En Vallaire at Saint-Sulpice near Lausanne VD is a special case where the skeletons of a man and a woman (the latter had been killed by an axe-blow on the back left parietal) were found disturbed; this calls to mind the rite of secondary flesh removal. Insufficient information makes it impossible to estimate the social differentiation which must have existed in funerary practices.

TRANSALPINE SWITZERLAND DURING THE EARLY BRONZE AGE

Plate 31

Though there is not the total and inexplicable blank already mentioned for the Neolithic period, the evidence from the Tessin and the Swiss valleys of the Po basin during the Bronze Age is still very scanty. Indeed, it is again noticeable and disappointing to see that a short distance from the Polada culture centres (lake- and moor-dwellings on the southern sides of neighbouring lakes: lake Maggiore, lake Como), and also the more numerous ones around lake Garda, hardly anything similar is found. The most reliable evidence is a dwelling floor uncovered at Carasso near Bellinzona TI, in the Ticino valley, which presumably belongs to the Polada culture. Dry-stone foundations are all that remain of the building. This very low human density must result from the impossibility of exchanges through the Saint-Gothard pass at this period. But this does not explain why Poladian groups did not try to colonize the lower part of the Tessin canton.

CONCLUSIONS

Between 1900 and 1500 BC the Swiss Early Bronze Age is characterized by its relative wealth, especially in metal which should be linked to the exploitation of copper sources scattered in several regions of the Alps. This represents a prosperous period for these regions, which is clearly demonstrated by the abundance of finds, mostly metal artifacts, gathered mainly in the Valais. The presence of the Bell-Beaker people in the Valais certainly provided a solid foundation for the establishment and development of the Rhône-Alpine culture. Moreover, influences from Central Europe (Hungary, Bavaria) show that techniques and ideas, and probably also men, were scarcely hindered by natural obstacles. In the case of the Plateau other Central European influences were felt which added to the wealth of the indigenous culture which derived from those of the Late Neolithic.

CHAPTER VI

The Middle Bronze Age

Fig. 25

There is less to say about the Middle Bronze Age in Switzerland. First, it is of shorter duration than the Early Bronze Age (from the fifteenth to the thirteenth centuries BC), and second it is known mostly from burials and isolated artifacts which restricts our knowledge of daily life. Furthermore, the features of this age are not very distinctive and there is no clearcut break with the Early Bronze Age, as the continuity of settlement shows. In the Alpine territory at least there is a sequence of dwelling levels from the Early Bronze and through the Middle Bronze Age or part of it, and even later. The features of the preceding period do not disappear but evolve as much by natural processes as by changes in the currents of influence. Indeed, these influences still originate in Central Europe but come from a different region and culture. The Únětice (Aunjetitz) sphere recedes and gives way to Hungarian and Romanian groups. There is no reason to think that this cultural influence was carried by migrating tribes.

A phenomenon occurs which partly contradicts what has just been said about continuity in site occupation and which poses a difficult problem: the complete break in the habitation of lake- and moor-dwellings not long after the beginning of the Middle Bronze Age. Two exceptions are striking: the Baldegg LU and Bleiche (Arbon TG) lake-dwellings where the beginning of the Middle Bronze Age is still present. It is impossible to explain this abandonment of the shore villages by climatic change. Indeed, in the deposits containing the remains of the last Early Bronze Age villages as well as in those lying above them, and also in the pollen diagrams, there is no indication of a change in the degree of humidity or in the precipitation which could have resulted in a rise in the water-level or a change in the vegetation. It is true that palaeobotanists have indicated that mixed oak forests gave way to beech during the Bronze Age (which corresponds to the Sub-Boreal), but this is not enough to justify the phenomenon.

Perhaps it can be explained by human causes possibly connected with changes in the methods of exploiting the environment. The breeding of cattle, sheep, and goats may have become more important. However, the fact remains that the density of Middle Bronze Age finds is still important around at least some of the lakes and away from the shores.

As before, settlers were attracted by hill-tops and sometimes also by caves, for example the site at Saint-Brais (Glovelier BE) which indicates quite a deep penetration into the Jura. Sites on steep hills in the Alpine region or nearby are well known, for instance Le Burg on Spiez BE which dominates both lake Thoune and the Simmental pass (the entrance to the Bernese Oberland). The other Early Bronze Age sites already mentioned are those of the Grisons canton at Cresta (Cazis), Mutta (Fellers) and Crestaulta (Lumbrein). The architecture of the houses hardly differs from that of the preceding period.

THE PLATEAU AND THE JURA

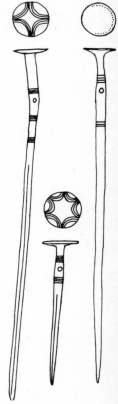

The distinction between the Alpine zone and the rest of the country (with the exception of the Tessin) continues but is not so clear. On the Plateau transition was peaceful, for there are still typical artifacts from the beginning of the Middle Bronze Age in two lake-dwellings at Bleiche (Arbon TG) and Baldegg (Hitzkirch LU). But only isolated artifacts have been found from this first phase. A pin is worthy of mention. Its stem is quadrangular in section and it has a flat head and perforated neck. This derives from a type known in lower Austria and Hungary and called the Regelsbrunn pin. There are also other types of pins with perforated necks. One with a triangular perforated head or lyre-head is presumably of indigenous origin. Among the weapons there is a sword with a long slightly curved blade and wide base, as well as flanged shouldered axes.

For the second phase, there is the group of barrows or tumuli at Weiningen (Plate 32) where the funerary material is most important. The eastern influences already mentioned brought to the Swiss Plateau the rite of depositing both the body (sometimes cremated) and accompanying objects under barrows. This is why the name 'tumulus period' was at first given to the Middle Bronze Age. This seemed to be justified considering not only Switzerland where barrows are rare, but the whole area of which it is a part together with southern Germany and eastern France. But despite the region of origin this name is still perhaps

Fig. 29 Middle Bronze Age; pins with discoid head and square stem, Valangin NE; Vully-le-Bas FR, Sugiez; Mörigen BE. Max. length c. 14.3 cm

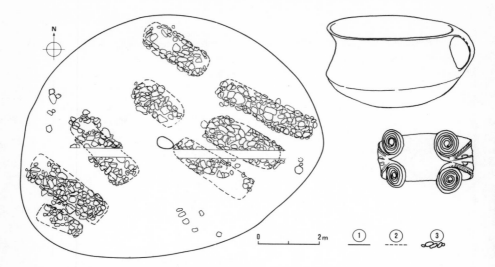

Fig. 30 *Middle Bronze Age; Weiningen level; Weiningen ZH; plan of the graves in barrow 3.* 1, *approximate limit of the barrow;* 2, *outlines of the graves;* 3, *stones on the graves. At right: pottery and bronze armlet (to same scale) from other barrows; ht. of pot c. 8 cm*

ill-chosen as it could suggest that one group had replaced another, which is not the case. Specialists retain it by force of tradition and for convenience.

Swiss barrows are very flat, which explains why agriculture has destroyed many of them. They have no well-defined borders, which might be because they were built at different periods so that they expanded each time a burial was added. Building materials are of clay and stones.

The Weiningen barrows which covered several tombs sealed by stone blocks have a considerable number of personal ornaments, mostly of bronze, which are characteristic of the second phase. The most beautiful are spiral leg-guards, extremely rare in Switzerland, which derive from Hungaro-Romanian types. In addition there are finely carved pins with round sections, fairly wide heads and perforated necks, and spiral wired tubes, etc. The use of amber should be noted.

Weapons include swords and daggers with a trapezoidal base with two or four rivets, and axes which are not very different from those of the previous phase. The heavier ones were certainly used as tools.

Fig. 31 *Middle Bronze Age; Weiningen level; perforated pins from Zurich, Cortaillod NE, Niederhasli ZH. Max. length c. 14.3 cm*

To help define the third and last Middle Bronze Age phases, there are on the whole only either isolated objects or those in deposits; tombs are rare. The distribution of certain types shows a geographical differentiation to which it would be imprudent to give an ethnic meaning. In the evolution of the bronze pins (when the perforated neck disappears) there is a form with transverse ribs in relief on the neck and head; this type is restricted to western Switzerland which has this feature in common with eastern France. As the evolution progresses the relief of the ribs is emphasized, ultimately producing the disc-headed pin. The sword is longer (up to 0·70 m) and narrower. Its wide and more rounded base is fixed into a haft which might sometimes be made of bronze, carefully ornamented with engravings; this is a south German type which is always rare. The dagger also evolves: the blade is more squat and the central rib sometimes has grooves on either side. Amongst the tool equipment only flanged axes are known, with a larger and rounder cutting edge, and sickles of a knobbed type.

Plate 33

THE ALPS

It would be even more difficult than for the Early Bronze Age to draw a precise line between the groups living in the Plateau and the Jura and those in the Alpine valleys during the Middle Bronze Age. There were movements in both directions (the introduction of cultural traits from the Plateau into Bernese Oberland, for example) as well as exchanges which the existence of passes must have encouraged. Transalpine influence was important and contributed to the traditional individuality of the Alpine province. This province is not homogeneous, however, and two zones may be distinguished: the Valais and the Grisons.

In the Grisons are the only sites examined in detail (Cazis, Fellers and Lumbrein). In the Lumbrein commune, the Crestaulta site stands next to a cemetery (Cresta Petschna) which has revealed objects of great importance. There are tombs containing cremations without a barrow, clustered around a stone block; the presence of ornaments alone could indicate that this was the part of the cemetery reserved for women. A large hearth and animal bone deposits give an insight into the rites practised there.

Fig. 32

The Grisons have revealed a structure of another kind related to religious practices, providing a valuable indication of the exploitation of

Fig. 33

underground resources by this population of shepherds. A case in point is the wooden double well at the Mauritius spring, Saint-Moritz GR. The healing properties of this water were appreciated by people of the fourteenth and thirteenth centuries BC who considered it important enough to hold sacrifices there. This is proved by two fine swords with solid bronze hilts which had been fixed vertically in the ground along with a dagger and a ribbed pin. A blade dated to the beginning of the Late Bronze Age shows the continued use of this spring which was known internationally by the end of the Middle Ages.

A short cultural history of the Alpine Middle Bronze Age can be established by taking into account all these kinds of sites as well as isolated finds, and what is best known in the neighbouring regions. The essential feature of the first phase is, as already stated, a continued tradition from the Early Bronze Age. This fact, along with the presence of objects from the Plateau (grave-goods at Varone VS with sword and pins, for example), does not define this initial phase very precisely.

The second stage is hardly clearer in the Valais. On the contrary, thanks to the Cresta Petschna cemetery (Lumbrein GR) it is easier to perceive the indigenous Early Bronze Age tradition (pins clumsily

Fig. 32 Middle Bronze Age in the Alps; Surin GR, Cresta; pins and other ornaments from graves. Longest pin c. 11 cm

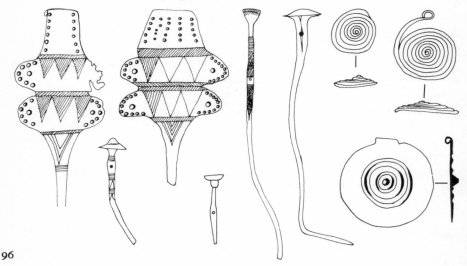

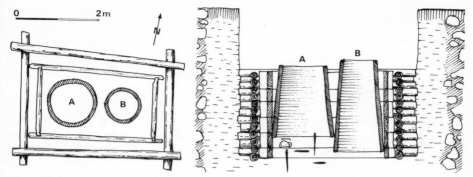

Fig. 33 Middle and Late Bronze Age in the Alps; Saint-Moritz GR; the sacred wooden wells of Saint Mauritius. At the bottom of the well at left are the offerings: rapiers, fragment of a sword blade and a pin

copied from the double trefoil ones) and the cultural contribution of the Plateau and of more distant countries (southern Germany and Austria, sheet-bronze pendants with circular decoration and button). Elsewhere a type of open bracelet, distributed from the Valais (Saxon) as far as the Saint-Gallese Rhine (Mels SG) and the centre of the Grisons (Savognin, 1225 m high), seems characteristic of the Alpine region, in spite of south German examples. A very narrow axe and an axe with an oval cutting edge are other examples.

The pottery of the Grisons is better known than that of the Plateau. It comes mostly from Crestaulta and Cazis and is characterized by wide forms and above all by plastic decoration made of thin cords on the girth, sometimes wavy and sometimes ribbed. Pieces of pottery with excised decoration were also found indicating a southern influence.

The last phase of the Middle Bronze Age hardly differs from what is known from the Plateau. The most characteristic finds from the Saint-Moritz double wall are significant. The conservatism of these mountain peoples is overcome little by little by the economic and cultural impact of their northern neighbours.

THE TESSIN

Only one find, probably funerary, at Gordola, north of lake Maggiore, testifies to life in Transalpine Switzerland at this period. The pairs of bracelets and pins found here are related as much to northern Italy as to the groups of the northern Alpine range.

CHAPTER VII
The Late Bronze Age

The transition *c.* 1250 BC between the Middle Bronze and the Late Bronze Age corresponds to a confused period in Europe, especially in the east. It is a period of migratory movements, mainly from north to south, of which the last reported by history are the Dorian invasions in Greece and the naval incursions of the 'Sea-Peoples' in the eastern Mediterranean. These more or less violent ethnic movements naturally had repercussions, mainly towards the west. The result was a huge circulation sometimes of human groups (not real invasions) but above all the circulation of ideas and influences which were already evident during the Middle Bronze Age. Switzerland also felt the effects, even though archaeologists now tend to minimize the migratory element.

The most noticeable consequence of these repeated movements from an archaeological point of view is the introduction of a new funerary rite: cremation with ashes deposited in urns grouped in cemeteries. This gave rise to the expression 'Urnfield culture' which is often used to denote this period. In fact, in Switzerland only the first phases of the Late Bronze Age are well provided with urnfields; this label can be applied to the whole culture only by analogy with neighbouring countries. As these burials contained quite a number of objects there is important archaeological evidence. Moreover, there are other classes of material as a result of the revival of the shore settlements (lake-dwellings) which increase in the second part of this period and become important centres of a rich culture. Unfortunately, these lake-dwellings, discovered more than a century ago, were not systematically investigated – apart from a few more recent ones – and the mass of objects they yielded must now be analyzed typologically in order to draw cultural and chronological conclusions, with all the risks of error that this entails.

Many attempts were made to classify the phases of the Late Bronze Age, with those of the German school making matters even more complex. It is not our concern to illustrate all the subtleties of this classification here. It is usually assumed, however, that the term 'Late Bronze Age' applies not only to the last stage of the Bronze Age proper

(P. Reinecke's Bronze D), which is close to the Middle Bronze Age, but also to the first two stages of Hallstatt (Ha A and B). This clearly demonstrates how arbitrary the chronological limits in archaeology are, and it is understandable that some prehistorians have preferred to rework this scheme by distinguishing the phases of the Bronze Age (the last stages of which are called E⁄F; V. G. Childe, C. Hawkes), or else by dividing it according to successive numbers (J. Déchelette, I–IV; J. J. Hatt, Early Bronze I–III; Middle Bronze I–III; Late Bronze I–III). We have nevertheless followed the German system which is generally used in Switzerland. This considers as Late Bronze the epoch (Bronze D and Ha A⁄B) which merits the name 'Urnfield' period. This represents a duration of five hundred years, from *c.* 1250 to 750 BC.

By including in the Bronze Age the beginnings of what has been termed Hallstatt, it can be assumed that the use of iron had quietly appeared. It will be seen later what this means. The first stage of this culture which blossomed all over Europe will be discussed with its economic wealth, technological inventions, effective socio⁄political organization and cultural grandeur. Switzerland benefited from this development, either because certain small groups had settled in the fertile regions of the Plateau or because the communities between the Jura and the Alpine valleys had received these innovations by exchange or in other ways. At certain periods during these five hundred years Switzerland was under the rule of feudal chiefs from southern Germany or eastern France, though this does not imply population movements.

We will see that Switzerland not only received but also took advantage of the new techniques (mainly in bronze and pottery) and the socio⁄political organization to develop several centres of economic and artistic influence within its territory. Everything indicates that there was no break in settlement in Switzerland around the thirteenth century BC, merely a smooth transition.

THE FIRST PHASES OF THE LATE BRONZE AGE

The transition from the Middle Bronze Age is clearly demonstrated by the occasional persistence of the rite of inhumation beside the predominant rite of cremation. Funerary equipment is often abundant, except for pottery which is fortunately provided by the settlement sites.

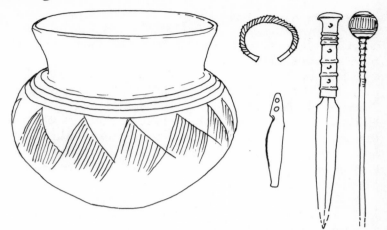

Fig. 34 Beginning of the Late Bronze Age or Urnfield culture; Mels phase; Mels SG, Heiligenkreuz; urn, ribbed bracelet, single- and double-bladed daggers and poppy-headed pin from a cremation grave. Ht. of urn c. 20 cm

A detailed typological analysis of the groups of objects discovered in the Swiss burials of this period and in those of neighbouring countries (southern Germany and eastern France) has made it possible to establish a sequence of two phases at the beginning of the Late Bronze Age, between *c.* 1250 and 1000 BC.

Fig. 34

The first phase can be classified under the Mels-Rixheim group (Mels SG; Rixheim, Haut-Rhin F). The most distinctive types are, in the case of bronze implements, the so-called 'poppy-headed' pin, the collared pin (derived directly from the transversally ribbed pin of the end of the Middle Bronze Age), a wire double-spiral S-hook, a bracelet with transversal ribs in relief, a knife with a single cutting edge (the first appearance of this weapon/tool in Europe), several kinds of tanged or solid-hilted daggers and finally the so-called 'Rixheim' sword which follows the Middle Bronze Age tradition with a two- or three-riveted tang projecting from the blade. The finds belonging to this group are unequally distributed which makes it difficult to characterize this phase any better. For instance, it is possible that the collared pins are earlier than the poppy-headed pins.

Pottery is known from a few rare finds (Zurzach ZH, Wiedlisbach

*Fig. 35 Beginning of the Late Bronze Age or Urnfield culture; Binningen phase. Left:
pin of Binningen type (section shown c. 8 cm long); right: Zurzach ZH, pottery (ht.
c. 16 cm)*

BE, etc.). There are mixed forms and decoration reminiscent of the
Middle Bronze Age (excised patterns) together with innovations
(vertical grooves separating conical protuberances). Tombs and objects
belonging to the first phase have been noted all over the Plateau (e.g.
Basadingen, Glattfelden and Egg ZH; Wangen and Wiedlisbach
AG; and recently Vuadens FR). Strangely enough, the Rixheim sword
has not been found in western Switzerland. Other objects are more
widely spread and are consequently less significant.

The second phase of the Late Bronze Age is named after the Binningen group. It belongs to Hallstatt A, i.e. Ha A1. This name (after a burial
at Binningen BL) is also that of a pin with a subglobular head above
several projecting ribs. Moreover, this group is characterized by solid
bracelets with round sections and thickened terminals, the earliest type
of fibula (violin-bow or Peschiera fibula), different types of knives, the
medial flanged-axe and a sword with a flat curved tang ending with a
'ricasso' (carp's-tongue sword). The few vessels found in tombs are urns
with a wide girth and low slightly carinated pots decorated like the
forms just mentioned. Most of these objects are too widely spread to
provide any evidence for cultural zones. Cultural maps can, however,

Plate 34

Plate 35

Plates 36, 37
Fig. 35

point out distant connections, as is the case for a type of flat-tanged dagger with its regional variations; distributed from the Leman to the Rhine, it stretches from south-east Europe and Italy up to Scandinavia.

Dwellings, which are little known for these two phases, and burials for the whole of the Late Bronze Age will be discussed later.

The Alps

Little is known of the first two phases of the Late Bronze Age in western Alpine Switzerland; they are represented by only a few objects found along the Rhône valley. This is not the case farther east where investigations have been more active during the last few years and where there are settlements and burials. We have already briefly mentioned the important Mels SG tomb, astride the threshold uniting the Rhine valley to the lakes of Walenstadt and Zurich and thus to the Plateau. The fact that it is the only funerary site of the first phase of the Late Bronze Age increases its value. In addition there are remains in Liechtenstein (Schellenberg FL) and in nearby Vorarlberg in Austria and also finds deeper in the Grisons valleys. The contents of a bronzesmith's hoard discovered at Caschligns (Cunter or Conters GR) in Oberhalbstein, on the route through the Julier and Septimer passes, include a two-piece bronze mould for casting a medial winged-axe, an axe of the same type but from a different mould and a very narrow axe with elongated wings. Also noteworthy is the incomplete Rixheim sword which was dedicated to the spring of Saint-Moritz GR, mentioned in the section on the Middle Bronze Age.

An isolated sword, found at Wallabütz Alp 1930 m high on the mountain above Mels SG and far from any important route, is noteworthy for two reasons: first, it has a hooked tang of Cypriot type; second, it represents a very widely spread type which is found from Egypt to northern France and Austria, passing through the Balkans and Italy. It probably belongs to the Binningen phase and agrees with the presence of medial winged axes in the heart of the Swiss Alps, in the cantons of Schwytz and Unterwald. In the following period there is more complete data for the Alpine region.

Fig. 36 Beginning of the Late Bronze Age in the Alps; Mels SG; Wallabütz-Matt; hooked-tanged sword. Length c. 46 cm

The Tessin

Only a few tombs provide sound information about the features of the Late Bronze Age culture in southern Switzerland. On both sides of the

Alps a number of analogies in bronze ornaments and pottery justify a comparison between the north Italian Peschiera culture and Late Bronze D, as well as between the Proto-Villanovan culture and Ha A and also partly Ha B. Burials around Bellinzona (Gorduno, Claro, Arbedo-Cerinasca, etc.) and the northern bank of lake Maggiore (Locarno-San Jorio, Ascona) can be assigned to the first phase. A faint resemblance to the regions north of the Alps (analogies with Bavaria and eastern France) emphasizes the unity which this Tessin complex has with the large urnfields of northern Italy such as Appiano and Canegrate, 50 and 65 km away from Locarno respectively.

'Le bel âge du Bronze': this phrase, borrowed from nineteenth-century French-speaking Swiss archaeologists (Desor and Favre), expresses the abundance, wealth and high technical as well as artistic quality of the period which now follows. Chronologically speaking this is the Ha A2 and B phase of the Late Bronze Age, dated between *c.* 1100 and 800/750 BC. The apex of the Bronze Age is reached and finally evolves into true Hallstatt.

Unfortunately, the wealth of material is not proportionate to our knowledge. In fact, the tens of thousands of objects kept in Swiss museums and elsewhere were mostly collected without method during the last century from lake-dwellings. The result was, of course, a mixing of the finds to which only more recent typological analysis can bring some order. Recently, however, systematic excavations were undertaken, either underwater, as at Grosser Hafner (Zurich) and at Auvernier NE, or in the open as at Zug Sumpf ZG, or on hill-top sites (Montlinger-berg at Oberriet SG, Mottata near Ramosch GR, Wittnauer Horn at Wittnau BL, etc.). Consequently, the evolution of the Late and Final Swiss Bronze Age is now a little easier to understand.

The Plateau and the Jura
As a whole there is a great homogeneity in the culture of both these regions, though some slight differences indicate probable cultural subdivisions which could have corresponded to ethnic or tribal idiosyncrasies. This is the case for the large, hollow bronze bracelets, well engraved, which were especially popular in western Switzerland.

The dwelling and the village Wood is the chief building material for dwellings. When built on dry ground or on rock, as at Kestenberg near Möriken AG, there is a line of small log-cabins, of which the most important is 5 × 6 m. They were built on a slope and one part had to be supported by poles, forming a half-pile house as is still to be seen in mountainous countries. But it is the lake-dwellings which illustrate the skill of Swiss builders from the eleventh to the eighth centuries BC. The house itself was very modest. At Zug Sumpf ZG, some houses were investigated which had two levels. In the first level (beginning of Ha B) there were huts with frames of vertical poles, the ends of which were fixed into a base with a plano-convex section, to prevent them from sinking into the damp ground. In the upper level (end of Ha B) there were square log-cabins, one 2.60 m long and another 3.20 m. These may be structures intended to support a more important upper floor. Carpenters had acquired much knowledge: how to cut wood, and how to use beams fixed by mortise and tenon.

Plate 38

An agglomeration is more interesting than a single dwelling. Aerial photographs taken above lake Neuchâtel along the north-west bank have brought to light several villages protected by 3 or 4 m of water. They present an extraordinary regularity: parallel streets, huts lined like cottages in England, and a fence which is generally incomplete and either faces the lake or stands on the side of the present bank. The first photograph of such an urban complex was taken at Cortaillod in 1927 but it went unpublished for a long time. During the last few years Michel Egloff has had the opportunity to photograph (weather permitting) half a dozen villages, and this is only the beginning.

There is, therefore, a lot of information, not only on architecture and urbanism but also on social organization. The latter would have been somewhat hierarchical in order to allow the setting-up of a village according to an enforced and strict plan. The impression is also given of a relatively dense human population along the ancient banks of the lakes. Although the short-lived settlements had to be rebuilt quite frequently, nevertheless the prosperity, proved by the wealth of archaeological material, was accompanied by an increase in population and settlements.

The hill-top settlements were protected by fortifications. G. Bersu has carefully investigated those at Wittnauer Horn (Wittnau BL) and has reconstructed a wall 12 m high on a base 30 m wide.

Crafts   In these villages there are several indications of work organized according to specialization. At the lake⁄dwelling sites of Les Eaux Vives at Geneva and Mörigen BE, for example, metal⁄workshops were localized, as is shown by moulds, fragments of bronze objects and waste metal; at Geneva there was also a butcher's store. At Auvernier NE there is a metal⁄workshop. At Landeron NE (not far from La Tène) a pottery workshop is attested with about 500 vessels while at the French site of Sévrier on lake Annecy (Haute⁄Savoie) there are the remains of a large kiln.

The activity of the bronze craftsmen was intense judging by the amazing quantity of objects they made. Tools became diversified and others were invented: wing⁄ended axes and adzes, new socketed chisels and gouges, hammers and anvils (also innovations), hooks and harpoons, saws, razors, sickle⁄blades whose wooden hafts are skilfully carved to protect the fingers, and finally the tanged or solid⁄hilted knives

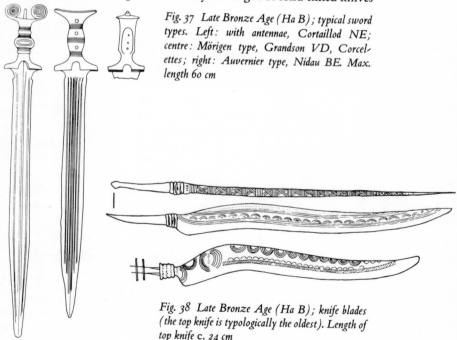

Fig. 37   Late Bronze Age (Ha B); typical sword types. Left: with antennae, Cortaillod NE; centre: Mörigen type, Grandson VD, Corcel⁄ettes; right: Auvernier type, Nidau BE. Max. length 60 cm

Fig. 38   Late Bronze Age (Ha B); knife blades (the top knife is typologically the oldest). Length of top knife c. 24 cm

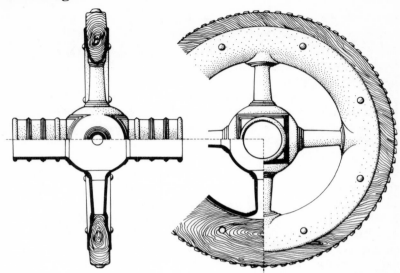

*Fig. 39 Late Bronze Age (Ha B); Cortaillod NE; reconstruction of the crushed
bronze and wooden wheel of a cult-chariot. Diameter of metallic felly 47.5 cm. Redrawn
with modifications after H. Buss, 1952*

Plate 39

Fig. 37

Fig. 39

which are one of the specific traits of the equipment of this period. The
arms-maker produced swords and spearheads of high quality. Swords
with long blades generally have a solid bronze hilt of variable shape.
There is the Mörigen sword (with a flat pommel), the Auvernier sword
(with straighter shoulder and a conical pommel) and the antennae
sword, all belonging to Ha B. The socketed spearhead, which is often
engraved, and the tanged or socketed arrowhead are frequent, while the
dagger disappears. Does this indicate a change in war techniques in
keeping with the development of horse-riding (horse-bits are present)
and the chariot? Or does it mean that the knife had taken the place of the
dagger?

The bronzesmith's skill is clearly demonstrated by the small wheel
from Cortaillod NE on lake Neuchâtel; it is a real masterpiece. Its study
has led to the analysis of the technique of manufacture: the elongated
axle, the hub with four spokes and the rim, open in a rounded V, were

cast in one piece before an oak tyre was added fixed by eight nails. The diameter was probably 0·50 m. The cauldron with spiral decoration found at Corcelettes VD is another example of the indigenous metalworkers' mastery. This luxury container is of an unmistakable northern type. But contrary to the generally accepted theory, D. Höckmann has recently demonstrated that it was not imported but is more likely the product of a Swiss craftsman who had almost perfectly imitated a foreign model.

The most important metal production in any quantity is of personal ornaments. Certain objects did not last long which is important from a chronological point of view. Bracelets, either solid with a ribbed decoration or hollow and engraved, were made with special care. There is a great variety of pendants. Pins are the most plentiful and offer greater variety. The most typical are those derived from the Binningen (Ha B2) type, the pin with bosses which lasted longest, the finely engraved globular hollow-headed pin with perforations (Ha B1) and the range of vase-headed pins, which are the latest (Ha B2).

At the very end of the Late Bronze Age the first iron objects appear, either alone (the Mörigen sword, the Nidau BE spearhead and the Saint-Aubin NE knife) or as a decorative element (damascening of bronze implements, etc.). This new metal was still a luxury.

The potter was not at all inferior to the bronzesmith. In spite of the absence of the wheel he or she was skilful enough to manufacture very fine vessels of black or grey ware. At first (Ha A2) forms with sharp profiles and high necks predominate probably imitating metal models;

Fig. 40 Late Bronze Age (Ha B); bronze bracelets from lake-dwellings on lake Neuchâtel, 1–2, Auvernier NE; 3, Concise VD. Ht. of (1) c. 9 cm

Fig. 41 Late Bronze Age (Ha B): Geneva, lake-dwelling of Les Eaux-Vives; pin with globular hollow-head. Length c. 20 cm

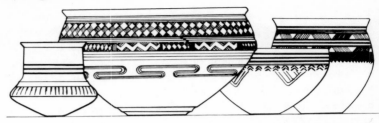

Fig. 42 Late Bronze Age; Zug Sumpf; pottery from the two levels. Left: Ha A; centre and right: Ha B. Max. ht. c. 15 cm

Plate 42, *Fig. 43*

then round bellied profiles with low neck (Ha B) evolve. The beauty of the vessel or plate is accentuated by the polishing of its surface and the

Plate 43

decoration. The latter is at first simple (Ha A3: incised lines and geometric motifs) but becomes more elaborate in the following phase with checkered patterns, symmetrical meanders and horizontal grooves outlining the bases of the handles. This has been called the 'rich style' which was at its best in painted pottery. It is monochrome (graphite pottery) and polychrome (black and red); there is also white inlay or, more noticeably, affixed tin bands forming ornamental motifs. This is the final phase of the Late Bronze Age (Ha B2) which some archaeologists prefer to consider as the very beginning of the Early Iron Age (Hallstatt).

Thanks to the pile dwelling sites, where a great number of objects made of organic material have been preserved, it is possible to include specialist woodworkers among the craftsmen. There are numerous examples of their technical capabilities. A clear idea of their ability is given by recent excavations at Auvernier NE where wooden containers have been discovered, shaped with a knife, which are of an astonishing regularity and beauty.

Plate 44

Basketry is represented at Auvernier by several dozen baskets in excellent condition. They are made according to the twilled technique which is still used today by basket makers.

Trade During the Late Bronze Age Switzerland was no more isolated than before; on the contrary it was included in the large cultural areas of southern Germany and eastern France. With and through these areas Switzerland established commercial relations which the use of chariots

Fig. 43 Late Bronze Age (Ha B); Möriken AG, Kestenberg; pottery. Max. ht. c. 17 cm

and horses as well as large canoes made easier. From the north came amber and the beautiful engraved and embossed sheet-bronze objects which the indigenous craftsmen tried to imitate. From the south, especially from Italy, an increasingly active stream brought characteristic objects such as the large Mörigen crested fibula. This implies that those crossing the Alpine passes of the Valais and the Grisons would not have come up against the hostility of the natives.

Religion   There is as yet no indication of the presence of a ritual building in a settlement. In fact, most of our knowledge on the non-material aspects of this civilization is based on burials. We must at this point repeat a question already posed when dealing with the Neolithic. In Switzerland there is no cemetery which is related to a site. This is particularly so in the case of lake-dwellings. It might be asked, therefore, whether these cemeteries lie between the villages and the present shore not yet covered by water.

The known burials are seldom clustered in great numbers. The practice of cremation and the depositing of ashes in urns is no longer the exclusive method as other rites are introduced. The example of the ten Boiron tombs (Tolochenaz, near Morges VD) is significant. They are scattered in a disorderly manner without round-barrows, and can be divided into two categories. On the one hand, there is cremation with an isolated urn (only one contained ashes) or with a group of pots, and in two cases there is a coffin made of slabs. On the other hand, there is inhumation of the body stretched out on its back with no urn or accompanying vessels. Apart from the pottery funerary goods consist of personal ornaments and pieces of animal bones. A chariot burial a few

Fig. 44

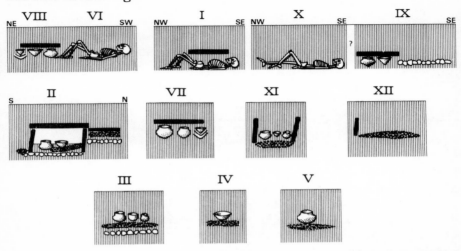

Fig. 44 Late Bronze Age; Tolochenaz VD, Le Boiron; cemetery with various funerary rites (inhumations, cremation in urn(s), with or without slabs). Redrawn after F. A. Forel, ASA, *1908*

kilometres farther away (Saint-Sulpice VD) may also be mentioned. There are two other examples of chariot burial at Berne-Kirchenfeld BE and Kaisten AG, foreshadowing those which would mark the Plateau during the Hallstatt period.

Plate 49
Fig. 45
Plate 45

Religious beliefs can also be deduced, though not very clearly, from personal ornaments and from symbolic decorative motifs. The sun is represented (wheels, discs, etc.) with its animal attributes (horse, swan or duck) and the crescent moon. The latter seems to have played an important part, judging from clay representations of it which are often richly decorated. Were these fire-dogs or cult objects? Taking into account north European evidence, one might wonder whether the small bronze and wooden wheel from Cortaillod was part of a ritual solar chariot.

The Alps

The Rhône valley   Only the last phase of the Late Bronze Age has been well identified in this area, either by deposits (Charpigny and Le Lessus,

Ollon VD, and lake Luissel, Bex VD) or by sites which unfortunately are poorly preserved (Le Lessus, Ollon VD, Collombey and Saint-Léonard VS). The influence of northern Italy is felt here.

The Rhine valley and the Grisons The main event east of the Swiss Alpine zone is the appearance of a new cultural group: this is the Melaun culture which is also found in the Austrian Tirol and north Italian Trentin. It is characterized mainly by its pottery: a jug with plastic incised decoration and a high handle with bosses at the top. This betrays Italian influences in this group which occupied the Rhine valley on its western boundaries nearly as far as lake Constance (Montlingerberg, Oberriet SG) and the Inn valley. Though this culture appears in the Late Bronze Age it is found up to the Roman conquest.

Plate 46

Plate 47

A group of monuments may be mentioned whose date is not yet known precisely, but which presumably belongs – or at least part of it – to the Bronze Age. These are the ten engraved rocks discovered in 1965 at Carschenna (Sils-im-Domleschg GR) near Thusis, at an altitude of about 1100 m. On the rocks are incised cup-marks, concentric rings, the sun, long wavy lines, horsemen, etc. Weapons or other objects are not represented and this makes chronological interpretation difficult. These petroglyphs present certain analogies with some of those at Val

Plate 48

Fig. 45 Late Bronze Age; Zurich, Alpenquai. Left: part of a bridle-bit depicting a horse (length c. 18 cm); right: detail of a pin or key with a bird, perhaps a duck (ht. of bird c. 3 cm)

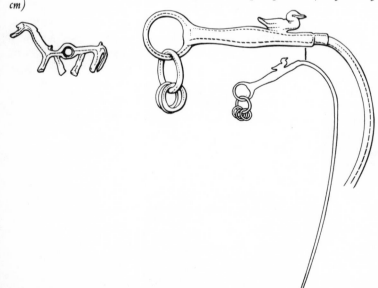

Camonica on the Italian side of the Alps, separated from Carschenna (as the crow flies) by only three passes (Julier or Albula, Bernina and Colle d'Aprica).

The Tessin

In this area there is no change from what has already been noted (page 103). The Tessin inhabitants are now part of the population and culture of northern Italy (Proto-Golasecca culture or Canegrate culture with influences from the southern proto-Villanovan). Further discussion must await the discovery of more settlements.

CULTURES AND ETHNIC GROUPS

Without entering into a complex debate the generally held opinions on the ethnic and thus also linguistic status of the Late Bronze Age inhabitants of Switzerland can be stated briefly. For several reasons the population of the Plateau and the Jura can be linked to the large community known as the Celts; the term proto-Celts has been put forward. The situation is less clear in the Alpine area. In the east it has been wisely proposed to assimilate the Melaun culture into the ethnic group of the Reti. According to E. Vogt the remaining Alpine population would probably have had no Indo-European links.

THE TRANSITION BETWEEN THE BRONZE AGE AND EARLY IRON AGE

The features of the culture which was long considered the last stage of the Late Bronze Age in the Plateau area can be interpreted in different ways, as already indicated. The continuity evident in phase Ha B is obviously important. Nevertheless, the appearance of iron as early as Ha B2 can be considered significant enough for it to be assumed that this is already Hallstatt. Moreover, if we take into consideration the influences from Italy, with all the late chronological links that entails, and if we assume that an important crisis could have taken place between Ha B1 and B2, with the construction of fortified sites, many deposits and a break in the extension of cemeteries, it is possible to maintain that the Ha B1-B2 division is more real than that between Ha B2 and Ha C. It is impossible, as far as our present knowledge goes, to advance anything other than only very uncertain hypotheses on the cause of this crisis. There is, however, a short transitional period during Ha B2.

CHAPTER VIII

Hallstatt or the First Iron Age Period

What has been said about the conventional break which separates the end of the Bronze Age and the beginning of the Iron Age leads quite naturally to the idea of the continuous development of economic life on the Swiss Plateau and in the Jura between at least the tenth and seventh centuries BC. If the beginning of the Hallstatt period is put at *c*. 750 BC, it lasts for three centuries ending *c*. 450 BC. There are two main stages: Early Hallstatt (Ha C in the adopted classification) which lasts to *c*. 600 BC and Late Hallstatt (Ha D) which can be subdivided into two phases (Ha D1 and D2, some authors adding Ha D3 which establishes the transition with the La Tène period).

The climatic crisis of 800 BC
This short period starts in peculiar ecological conditions. Indeed, about the ninth century BC (i.e. at the end of the Sub-Boreal) the climate underwent a crisis with severe consequences. Rain and humidity increased quite rapidly and caused a rise in the water-levels of rivers and lakes. The level of lake Geneva, for example, is estimated to have increased from 366 to 375 m (present level, 372 m). As for the lakes of Neuchâtel, Morat and Bienne, the variations in water-level were periodically influenced by changes in the course of the Aar, which, instead of continuing northwards, was obstructed by its own alluvium which drew it back to lake Bienne. This modification must have happened during the stage under discussion and accompanied the climatic phenomenon. This has been proved elsewhere: in the Saône basin, Alsace and southern Germany.

In any case, the lake- and moor-dwellings were abandoned; none are known definitely to have contained objects datable to Early Hallstatt. People living on the shores or in damp valley bottoms were compelled to search for higher sites on which to settle. This stir must have had serious consequences for the distribution of sites and the way of life. Another consequence is of direct interest for archaeologists: settlements are more difficult to detect. So far as the first Hallstatt phase is concerned, hardly anything is known about this aspect of human life and culture. During the second stage Hallstatt people colonized regions considered unattractive till then on account of their dryness. The high limestone plateaux of the Jura are a case in point.

The Hallstatt provinces

The transformation of the forests following the climatic crisis not only modified their composition, with beeches beginning to dominate in this Sub-Atlantic phase, but also accentuated their density and extent. Man counter-attacked by exploiting the forest and by sacrificing it for cultivatable land, but nevertheless it must have been an obstacle for trade. This is perhaps one of the explanations for the increased cultural fragmentation at the beginning of the Early Iron Age. Indeed, geographical subdivisions are attested whose cultural pecularities may have corresponded to ethnic and tribal realities. Pottery is most characteristic of this individualization.

Two main provinces can be distinguished on the Plateau and in the Jura. The first, which is linked to southern Germany and Alsace, includes, broadly speaking, the territory between Bienne, Thoune, Lucerne and Saint-Gall. The second stretches into western Switzerland, between Thoune and lake Geneva and is related to the French zone. Strangely enough, this western province seems to stop at the valley of the Aubonne, a stream which flows into lake Geneva opposite Thonon. Farther south-west from this frontier there is a 'no-man's land' throughout the Early Iron Age which reaches the canton of Geneva. Is it mere coincidence that, much later after the Gallic Wars, the Aubonne delineates the northern boundary of the *Colonia equestris*, founded by Caesar for his veterans, with its capital at Nyon VD and, during the Middle Ages, of the Geneva diocese? In any case, the Geneva region has not yet yielded any evidence of the culture between the end of the Bronze Age and the beginning of La Tène, with the probable exception of a flat barrow near Versoix GE, recently excavated but with very poor material which is difficult to date.

The other subdivisions include the Alpine and Transalpine zones: the Valais, Engadine, eastern Switzerland (the Rhine valley and the foothills of the Alps) and finally the Tessin and the Mesolcina valley. The chronological phases in these regions are generally less clear.

Early Hallstatt (Ha C)

In the absence of any information on settlement sites, burials and their structure and contents must suffice to reconstruct the culture of this period. Fortunately there is much information on this subject. Barrows are scattered in entire cemeteries from the cantons of Schaffhausen (Hemishofen-Sankert with thirty-five barrows) and Thurgovie (Ermat-ingen, etc.) to the canton of Soleure (Subingen with twenty barrows), passing through the largest group at Unterlunkhofen AG (more than sixty barrows) – to deal only with the northern area. In the west, the Bernese groups of Jegenstorf and Grächwil are noteworthy and will be discussed further because of the quality of their tomb furniture as at Grossaffoltern (twenty barrows) and Anet (Ins). From here barrows are distributed along the foot of the Jura (Cressier-La Baraque and Valangin-Bussy NB, Baulmes VD, etc.), and through the Plateau (Cordast, Chattonaye FR). Unfortunately, many of these western barrows have been carelessly investigated long ago and often nothing is left; this is why our knowledge of this western province is so fragmentary.

The barrows are located on terraces or slopes and now generally stand in woods which have protected them. Their dimensions are sometimes large: up to 20 m in diameter with their present height reaching 3 m; the average size is about 10 m in diameter and 1.20 m in height. These are cremation barrows centred on the tomb itself, consisting of one or more urns containing the ashes together with other pots which hold provisions for the after-life. Sometimes the barrow was built on the site of the funeral pyre which provided ashes to cover the urns. There may also be several hearths, probably vestiges of the funeral ritual. Over the remains stands the tumulus built of earth or in the form of a central cairn which protects the urns and is covered with earth. The barrow is sometimes surrounded by a circle of stones or small slabs which earth fallen from the slope has generally hidden. It is impossible to describe here all the variations in the building process. Some of them have a different geographical distri-bution. At the very end of Late Hallstatt the barrow with chariot burial appears which will be discussed later.

In western Switzerland as well as in Franche-Comté there are inhumation barrows heralding a funerary rite which became important during the following stage throughout the Plateau and Jura. Payerne VD is one example.

Plate 50

As regards the tomb furniture, it is worth mentioning that in the northern group pottery is plentiful, varied and of excellent quality whereas in the west it is less abundant except in the Aar valley between Berne and Olten. In contrast, the western province is richer in metal objects, especially in bronze, which could be attributed to the persisting of Late Bronze Age techniques in this zone. In north-east Switzerland, however, bronze is rarer and was used only to manufacture slightly engraved cast objects; iron was employed more often.

The northern province   Pottery is divided into six main categories: the subglobular (or bellied) jar, with a high shoulder and inverted truncated neck (sometimes with a lid); the low-necked pot; the jug (with a handle); the deep plate; the splayed plate with ribbing; and the bowl. The first type is the most distinctive as it is not, unlike the others, directly derived from Late Bronze Age forms. Traditional elements are also clear in the decoration with persisting geometric motifs; but painted decoration is also favoured as well as black-slip and even an adaptation of the batik process – zones were covered with wax thus isolating the motifs which were to retain the original colour of the wall. Excision was also used. The whole of this pottery is closely related to the so-called 'Alb-Salem' pottery in southern Germany which indicates that the northern province is connected with this large area, at least by its cultural traits.

Iron is used with increasing frequency for weapons and tools. There are large flat-tanged swords whose type of bronze hilt with wide pommels is known elsewhere. At the end of the Ha C period the flat-tanged type is replaced by a short sword with an antennae hilt. In addition there are knives and arrowheads, and therefore the bow, completing the armoury. The lunate razor and toilet-case, both made of iron, complete the equipment. Bronze is used only for ornaments: bracelets and pins (these are restricted to the northern province). Lignite, which is used to make bracelets, enjoyed an ever increasing popularity from this period.

Finally, there are a few gold objects, which appear rather late in Early Hallstatt and seldom in this province. Worthy of mention, however, is a beautiful gold bowl (25 cm in diameter, 12.5 cm high, weight 910 g) which was found at Zurich Altstetten ZH. It is embossed with small round protuberances isolating schematic animal motifs and certainly had a cult function. Even if it was not imported from the south it clearly testifies to Mediterranean influence.

The western province The archaeological inventory here differs from the northern province. Pottery is not so well known though vessels from the Jegenstorf barrows together with those from the region between Berne and Soleure give a partial idea of what western potters were able to do. Pottery, less under south-German influence, was painted but more often black-burnished, and cords in relief were also common ornamentation.

Differences in the rest of the material are not very important between the two provinces except in the case of bronze which is used increasingly for harness-pieces and for ornaments. These become widespread during the following period and include bells, pendants, open rings with mid-ribs and above all the famous disc with concentric circles and a central boss. Worn either on the chest or on the stomach, this disc, which occurs more frequently later on, appears also in eastern France, testifying to connections between both sides of the Jura.

The barrows of Anet (Ins) and Jegenstorf BE have yielded gold jewellery: spherical pendants with fine granular designs, small chains, etc. These were certainly imported products, probably from Italian workshops (Etruscan?). Here we catch a glimpse of the commercial currents which crossed Switzerland and which were to intensify during the following period.

Plates 53, 54

Late Hallstatt (Ha D)

Here again, the break separating the different periods must not be taken too literally. In fact there is no hiatus and more than one group of barrows is known which began just before the end of Ha C and developed continuously to the beginning of Ha D, just as there are cemeteries where Ha D1 and Ha D2 are represented without interruption.

The population increased, encouraged by a flourishing economy, and small-holdings begin to appear, mostly in the north built on hill-tops or on well-exposed slopes. Pastoral communities increasingly colonized the foot-hills of the Jura and the grazing lands. The relative mobility of the tribal groups is probably explained by the need to protect

Fig. 46

the fertile lands which they had found. It is significant that several fortified sites of this period have been identified and investigated. The most important are Wittnauer Horn (Wittnau BL), where the ruins of the Late Bronze Age rampart were used as the base for a new one, and Burgenrain (Sissach BL), about 10 km from the Rhine. Both sites are surrounded by a dry-stone-walled rampart reinforced by an inner wooden frame where the slope was not so steep; it approaches the *murus gallicus*. On Wittnauer Horn, a rather narrow promontory settlement, the double defensive system (*vallum* and wall) is separated by a 'no-man's land' of 120 m. A cluster of small wooden houses were aligned around the area which had to be defended. In addition there was a central house. The population of such a fortified village is difficult to estimate; for Wittnauer Horn, covering six hectares, a total of 500 inhabitants has been proposed. For Burgenrain, whose extent is much bigger, neither the density nor the distribution of the houses is known. In the same region of the tabular Jura near the Rhine, there are other smaller fortified sites (such as Bönistein on Zeinigen AG). The grandeur of Heuneburg (Württemberg D) is still far away, with its Celtic-type enclosure which was at one point replaced by a brick wall on dry-stone-walled foundations, reminiscent of the Hellenic Mediterranean; we are also far from Mont Lassois (Châtillon-sur-Seine, Côte d'Or F) which overlooks the marvellous burial of Vix.

In western Switzerland investigations have not been so extensive and no parallel example can be drawn, except perhaps that of Châtillon-sur-Glâne (Posieux FR) one mile upstream from Fribourg. The topography and recent discoveries there raise the hope that an

Plate 51

Fig. 46 Late Hallstatt; Wittnau BL, Wittnauer Horn; reconstruction of the defence system. 1, main rampart; 2, advanced wall; 3, ditches; 4, dwelling zone. Redrawn after G. Bersu, 1945

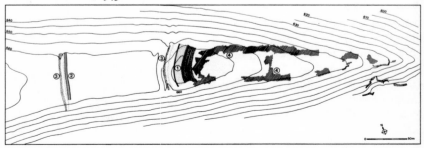

important fortified site will be found. Its location at the confluence of the Sarine and Glâne rivers and its name, almost meaning 'castle', hint at potentially rewarding excavations.

It is, therefore, too soon to draw a picture of the social, economic and political background of the whole of Switzerland between 600 and 450 BC. By analogy with neighbouring countries, especially southern Germany, we can assume there were local chiefs, either independent or paying tribute to more powerful princes, who ruled small territories. Those better located, i.e. those who had under their control important routes, commercial, agricultural or mining centres could acquire wealth, prestige and power. This is suggested by the size of numerous barrows and the quality of their contents.

Mines have already been mentioned. However, very little is known of the exploitation of mineral resources, except that it could not have been very important. Switzerland's subsoil is known to be poor. We have no proof that the iron in the Bernese Jura was extracted at this period though one can assume that it was exploited just as the iron in the much richer basin of eastern France was. There was gold in some of the rivers in the centre of the Plateau and the foothills of the Alps and we know from Posidonius that the Helvetii of the first century BC used to collect it. Such activity as early as the Hallstatt could explain the presence of gold jewellery in many barrows. It seems difficult, however, to envisage a source of raw materials there capable of creating an important trade.

It is probable that at least some of the gold objects found in Switzerland came from outside the country. They were part of the flow of influences and goods from the south, mostly from Italy. Oil and wine, when not transported in leather bottles, would reach the wealthy native patrons in containers made of sheet-bronze. Many of these were masterpieces from Etruscan or Greek workshops, magnificent works of art. The large hydria, deposited after 580 BC in a barrow at Grächwil BE and richly decorated with bronze motifs, is a case in point. The main decoration represents the 'mistress of the animals' with her companions (lions, hares, eagles and snakes). It is generally held that this remarkable piece, 0·64 m high, is from a workshop in Greater Greece (southern Italy). Plate 58

Traders succeeded even in bringing Greek pottery, some of which could not withstand the long and rough transportation. At Uetliberg

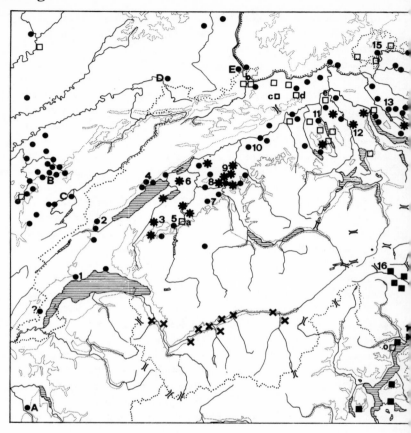

Plate 59

near Zurich, for example, a fragment of the handle of an Attic wine jar with red figures (palms) was found, dated to the beginning of the fifth century BC.

All these objects from the Mediterranean pose the problem of the route – or routes – they had to follow to reach the Swiss Plateau. The question of the larger crater (mixing bowl) from Vix in Burgundy has long been discussed. There are two conflicting hypotheses. For some, this huge vessel, transported in separate pieces, could only have reached Burgundy

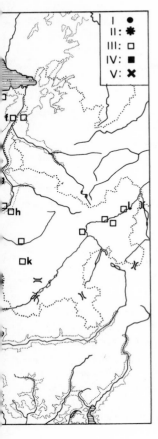

Fig. 47 Hallstatt (Early Iron Age). I, barrow (or group of barrows); II, barrow with chariot-burial (in Switzerland only); III, main settlements; IV, graves south of the Alps; V, other finds in the Alps and south of the Alps.
I, II and IV: 1, Aubonne VD; 2, Baulmes VD; 3, Payerne VD; 4, Valangin NE, Bussy; 5, Cormin-boeuf FR; 6, Anet-Ins BE; 7, Neuenegg BE; 8, Meikirch BE, Grächwil; 9, Jegenstorf BE; 10, Subingen SO; 11, Seon AG; 12, Unterlunkhofen AG; 13, Wangen ZH; 14, Hohentannen TG; 15, Hemishofen SH; 16, Quinto TI, Deggio; 17, Arbedo TI, Castione, Cerinasca, Molinazzo; 18, Minusio TI; 19, Rovio TI; 20, Ca'Morta I. France: A, Gruffy; B, groups of Salins-Moidons-Amancey; C, Pontarlier; D, Grandvillars; E, Blotzheim.
III: a, Posieux-Froideville FR, Châtillon-sur-Glâne; b, Muttenz BL; c, Sissach BL, Burgen-rain; d, Wittnau BL, Wittnauer Horn; e, Möriken AG, Kestenberg; f, Oberriet SG, Montlingerberg; g, Mels SG, Castels; h, Coire-Chur GR; i, Cazis GR, Cresta; k. Savognin GR; l, Ramosch GR; m, Mesocco GR; n, Castaneda GR; o, Ascona TI, Balla Drumme.
Thin dotted line: 700 m altitude

by way of the Rhône and Saône valleys; for others, the politico-economic situation in southern France (with the monopoly imposed by Massilia-Marseille) would have made the passage of precious goods destined for a Celtic tribe of the interior impossible at this time. The alternatives are the same for the Grächwil hydria. If the Rhône route is excluded, only the Transalpine route remains; in this case the Great Saint-Bernard pass (2469 m high) has first to be considered as it is the most direct; the Little Saint-Bernard pass is lower (2157 m high) and would have necessitated a longer detour. Both present serious difficulties but they were probably no worse for the seventh- and sixth-century traders than for those of the last century BC who left evidence of their passage. The eastern passes of Switzerland (San-Bernardino 2065 m; Splügen 2113 m, etc.) and those in Austria may also have been used.

Thus the existence of commercial traffic is established. If products were brought from Mediterranean workshops there would naturally have been exports from the Celtic principalities of the northern Alps. Gold and iron have been mentioned. Unlike neighbouring centres such as those at Salins in Franche-Comté, Hallein in Austria (Tirol) and the Hallstatt mines, Switzerland's sources of salt are too deeply buried to have been exploited at this time. We can assume instead that traders returned with cattle, hides, dried or salted meat and cheese, and occasionally with slaves.

Were the traders Greeks or were they, as is generally held, Etruscans who would have monopolized the function of intermediaries between the Alpine passes and the Mediterranean production centres? The Etruscan port of Spina on the Adriatic might have played an essential part in this trading.

Thus during the sixth and fifth centuries BC Hallstattian Switzerland experienced a civilization in which the indigenous traditions were deeply enriched by all these external contributions. Objects discovered testify to the presence of foreign trends and influences. Craftsmen acquired and perfected their techniques: jewellers imitated stippled designs on gold jewellery quite successfully, carpenter-masons built ramparts with a mastery reminiscent of foreign overlords, bronzesmiths quite skilfully imitated situlae and other containers imported from the south.

The Late Hallstatt culture

The external influences have been illustrated in order to emphasize the importance they acquired in the 150 years preceding the flowering of the La Tène civilization. The Late Hallstattian culture will now be described at least as regards those features not yet dealt with which differ from the previous period. Funerary structures are very important for the understanding of this culture and will be discussed first.

Burials　The main phenomenon to be mentioned is the smaller number of barrows of larger size. The rite of cremation continues to decline and gives way to inhumation, especially in the west of the country. But whereas the first inhumation barrows of Early Hallstatt were generally reserved for one person, now the custom develops of a collective barrow, or rather of a family barrow. Instead of a cluster of barrows, there is now only one with several primary burials to which secondary tombs were added (at Hemishofen SH, for example). Up to twenty tombs were counted in one barrow. The lack of proper records on early excavations restricts the scope of this description. At Seon AG, however, it is known that the two rites coexisted, with ashes and corpses separated by low dry-stone walls.

Grave-goods – often rich ones – accompanied the dead. Special mention should be made of a distinctive type of high-class barrow: the chariot-burial which is found in central and western Europe, from Bohemia to Burgundy and France-Comté. The Swiss Plateau and the southern slopes of the Jura near Neuchâtel have so far brought to light twenty examples. The earliest date from the end of Early Hallstatt (Ha C); the majority can be dated to the last phase of Late Hallstatt (Ha D2), i.e. between 500 and 450 BC. In these barrows either a complete chariot, with two or four disassembled wheels, or parts of chariots were deposited. Generally the hub of the iron wheels is best preserved. Remains of horse-trappings are also sometimes found, as at Anet (Ins) BE where pieces of leather decorated with bronze studs were recognized by A. Gansser-Burckhardt as ox or stag hide; the way the leather was tanned with vegetable products made him think that it came from the Danube or Balkan region.

Plate 55

The position of the chariot varies in relation to the corpse or to the ashes. These burials usually contained great wealth: large rings made of sheet-gold at Payerne VD and Châtonnaye FR, gold jewellery at Anet (Ins), Urtenen BE and Adliswil LU, bronze vessels (cauldrons, situlae or hydriae) at Rances VD, Châtonnaye and Guin (Düdingen) FR, Anet, Meikirch-Grächwil BE, Adliswil LU and Wohlen AG, etc., not to mention the less striking ornaments of all varieties. German archaeologists have put forward the term *Fürstengrab*, 'princely-burial', to indicate these wealthy barrows. This is perhaps acceptable but the word 'prince' should not be taken too literally. Nevertheless, the burials support the impression of a hierarchical society in which wealth was unequally distributed.

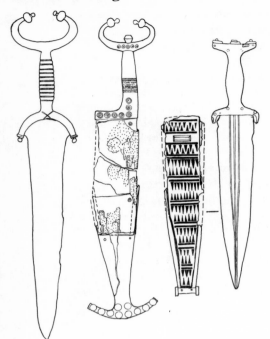

Fig. 48 Late Hallstatt (Ha D); daggers and scabbard. Left to right: from Sion VS, Neuenegg BE, Cudrefin VD. Length of dagger at left 43 cm

Crafts Pottery, always a reliable guide for social and technological evolution, loses its popularity during the Late Hallstatt period. Shapes are less accentuated, painting and excised patterns become rare. Among the characteristic types the vessel with high neck and wide girth may be mentioned along with cups and other small pots which increase. In inverse correlation to this impoverishment, bronze vessels become more numerous. On the other hand bronze gives way to iron for the making of weapons. The most characteristic are the long iron-tipped spear and dagger, and the dagger with asymmetrical hilt or antennae dagger, the successor to the sword·which has practically disappeared. The best preserved examples was found in lake Neuchâtel at Estavayer-le-Lac FR. Detailed technical examination showed that in this workshop masterpiece seventeen elements were needed besides the blade, and were held together by means of eleven rivets; twenty-five riveted elements were necessary to make the sheet-iron sheath.

Plate 56
Fig. 48

Plate 57

124

Personal ornaments reveal the growing wealth of the Hallstatt people during the second period. Bronze is the chief material used. The most characteristic ornaments in their approximate order of appearance are as follows. There are openwork discs with a central boss whose significance is unclear; these are limited to the beginning of Late Hallstatt (Ha D1) and are peculiar to the western province. The most easterly example is from Subingen SO and in France beyond the Jura. The bell-pendant is in fashion. A type of object appears from the south which puts an end to the popularity of the pin: the fibula, ancestor of our safety-pin. The arc fibula with an elongated terminal is the earliest, along with the boat-shaped (*navicella*) fibula with enlarged and decorated bow. Belts are ornamented with buckles of many different shapes.

Plates 61, 63

Fig. 49

Bronze wire torques, flat earrings and above all bracelets and armlets made of sheet-bronze appear a little later; among them the most striking are the barrelled armlets. A detailed analysis of the delicate decoration of these female ornaments has made it possible to distinguish regional variations. From the north-east to the south-west the boundaries of these variations can be indicated approximately by the following localities: Hemishofen SH – Brugg AG – Olten SO – Neuchâtel – Lausanne VD. The density is heaviest in the west and corresponds to what is found in neighbouring France.

The second Late Hallstatt (Ha D2) phase is characterized by the uniformity of the Swiss Plateau culture, together with the strong diversification of the types of objects. Fibulae in particular display remarkable imagination: serpentiform fibulae whose bow is twisted

Fig. 49 Late Hallstatt (Ha D) in N. Switzerland; evolution of the fibula. 1, Ha D 1, Lenzburg AG; 2, Ha D 2, Wittnau BL, Wittnauer Horn; 3–4, Ha D 2, Wohlen AG; 5–6, Ha D 3, Unterlunkhofen AG. After W. Drack, 1974. Max. length c. 6 cm

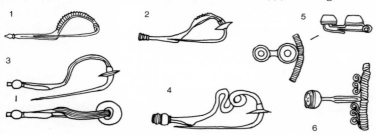

Plate 62

around itself from a disc; simple and double drum-shaped fibulae; and, towards the end of this period, cross-bow fibulae whose spring stretches laterally sometimes ornamented with small loops. The varieties of torques, bracelets and anklets increase. Belts have hooks and sheet-bronze plaques which differ according to region and sex of the wearer; women's are larger and decorated in repoussée. Among the pendants, those in basket and human form are noteworthy (Unterlunkhofen AG). Besides gold and bronze, all kinds of lignite (jet, etc.) were used to make bracelets which were broad with a rounded section.

This discussion has not emphasized typological and chronological aspects, but it is sufficient to show the wealth of the evolved Hallstatt culture. Some features foreshadow the La Tène culture and style: for instance, the bronze plaques with hooks which decorated the belts of individuals inhumed in the Vaud canton barrows at the very end of the Hallstatt period (Ha D3 of some authors). But before considering the transition from the first stage of the Iron Age to the second stage we must survey events between 750 and 450 BC outside the Plateau and the Jura.

THE WESTERN ALPS

A group of barrows has recently been discovered in the foothills of the Alps at Fribourg near Schwarzsee (Plaffeien FR), 1040 m high. Excavations have not yet begun and one can only note this important indication of penetration into Alpine territory, and put forward the hypothesis that this is a localized extension of the western province of the Plateau.

THE VALAIS

The little we know about the Valais from isolated objects shows that it differs little from the western Alps. The antennae dagger, openwork disc, armlet and lignite bracelet are present. In addition there are objects imported from northern Italy or from Tessin.

It was believed that the tribes living in the Valais at this period could be named by referring to Avienus, author of the *Ora maritima* (end of the fourth century BC). Taken from an author of *c.* 530 BC, there is a reference to the *Tylangii, Daliterni* and *Clahicli*. The non-Indo-European and non-Celtic sound of these names appeared to be significant. It seems, however, that in this case caution is necessary since the text quoted by Avienus, as well as his own, went through so many alterations before being transcribed in the first known manuscripts that these names are not only unreliable but may even not apply to people located upstream from lake Geneva.

The Melaun culture continued to evolve but could not withstand the impact of the Hallstatt culture spreading up the Rhine valley and the nearest Grisons valleys. At Tamins GR, a little upstream from Coire (Chur) in a large cremation cemetery containing sixty-three tombs without a barrow, an evolution can be traced towards more localized pot types. The first burials yielded pottery which can easily be linked to that of Alb-Salem in southern Germany, whereas in the later burials there are vessels with simplified forms and impressed decoration.

Plate 65

The influx from the south through the Alpine passes combined with the Hallstattian influence from the north to remove the characteristic features of the Melaun culture at the end of the Hallstatt period.

This region presents a different cultural milieu. As at the end of the Bronze Age, the Tessin canton and the Mesolcina valley belong culturally to northern Italy, i.e. to the Golasecca culture which was located in Lombardy. Those interested in a description of this culture should turn to L. Barfield's *Northern Italy before Rome* (1971); here we will only indicate what has been brought to light in Swiss territory. There are many burials which are sometimes clustered in a large necropolis like those around Bellinzona. The Cerinesca cemetery at Arbedo comprises 167 burials, including later ones, made directly in the soil without barrows.

In a 1970 publication Mrs M. Primas attempted to classify all the grave-goods of Italian Switzerland. The absence of weapons is a striking peculiarity. She has shown that the earliest settlement of the first Iron Age culture was only founded during the later phase of this period, i.e. at the end of Golasecca II (equivalent to Ha D2 in the northern Alps). There are three phases (Tessin A, B and C), dating from 550 to 450 BC. The

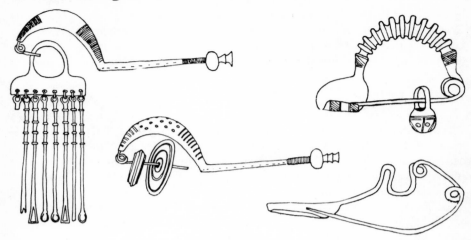

Fig. 50 Hallstatt south of the Alps (Tessin B); Arbedo TI, Cerinasca; fibulae. Left: two boat-shaped fibulae (navicella) with heavy foot; top right: ribbed fibula; bottom right: serpentine fibula. Max. length c. 12 cm

rite of cremation brought from neighbouring countries continues but inhumation is also introduced and it is impossible to understand the reasons for choosing between these two rites. In the former the cinerary bowl, later replaced by an urn, was put in a small coffin made of slabs. Objects were put on it and pottery beside it. In the case of inhumation the body was surrounded by stones or slabs with a covering of slabs. Vessels were placed at one end of the burial. A little later burials appear in which the urns or slab-tombs are placed in a square or a circular pit surrounded by a small dry-stone wall (e.g. Locarno-Minusio TI).

Grave-goods are generally plentiful and include pottery as well as personal ornaments worn by the deceased. The most characteristic vessels are the large pots with wide shoulders, decorated with pattern-burnished designs (*stralucido*) or horizontal cords in relief, low-footed bowls and high-necked beakers. Ornaments, mostly of bronze and some of iron, are sometimes decorated with coral and amber. There are ribbed boat-shaped or serpentiform fibulae, earrings with hooks, multiglobular-headed pins, discs, etc. The most distinctive ornament is the rectangular plaque of a belt, with repoussée decoration, which seems to have been

Plate 60

Fig. 50

Plate 69

reserved for men. This is strictly limited in time to the Tessin A-C phase and is found only in the Tessin valley, upstream from lake Maggiore. This might be a tribal peculiarity.

The relative equality which exists in the grave-goods of the Tessin cemeteries gives the impression of a less hierarchical population than that of the Swiss Plateau. Very rare chariot-burials (*carettino*) in nearby Lombardy (Sesto Calende, Como-Ca' Morta and Como-Rebbio) are exceptions which do not contradict this idea, which in any case is based only on funerary evidence. The Tessin population had probably taken part of its wealth from the Transalpine trade. Indeed it was wide open to the main influences which crossed the north Italian plain, mainly those coming from the east, from the Veneto and even from farther afield. But Etruscan influence also begins to be felt; trade with the Hallstatt principalities began at the end of the sixth century and reached its peak from 500 BC onwards. Among the finds from Tessin at this period, mentioned briefly when discussing products imported on the Swiss Plateau, are fragments of oenochoes (flagons) of Etruscan origin or made in imitation of models from Etruscan workshops (the bronze hoard and grave-goods at Molinazzo-Arbedo and Pazzalo near Lugano TI). There is, however, no sure chronology as far as these are concerned. In fact, in the low valleys of Italian Switzerland a trend begins which will carry luxury goods northwards in the following period.

CHAPTER IX

La Tène or the Second Iron Age Period

The La Tène style

It has often been shown that the transition between the first and second stages of the Iron Age was neither abrupt nor caused by sudden invasions, but that it corresponds mainly to a cultural change given artistic expression. Metal ornamentation evolved quite rapidly within two generations under the influence of works of art imported from the Mediterranean Classical world and of craftsmen from the same area. It is highly probable that these bronzeworkers and jewellers benefited from the encouragement and hospitality of the principalities which continued the feudal Hallstatt tradition. The result was a very distinctive decorative art whose sources of inspiration are mostly flower motifs popular with the Greeks and their Etruscan imitators; the chief pattern is the palmette. In addition, inspirations came from the east, from the horsemen of the steppes (Scythians, Cimmerians and the Medes and Persians) and from the south-west, i.e. Iberia. This style contrasts with that of Hallstatt which is very geometrical and rigid. There are many variations of plant motifs, and it combines curves and spirals in a symmetrical association. This La Tène style spread all over Celtic Europe, all the more easily since there was a relatively homogeneous ethnic background. This rapid evolution involved Switzerland directly.

The evidence of history

La Tène marks the entrance of the Celtic world into history. At the beginning of the period the importance of this should not be exaggerated. Indeed, the records of ancient Greek and Roman authors are rare and unreliable for Early and Middle La Tène, i.e. between 450 and 200 BC, nor do they provide much more information than archaeology does. If one considers only the area which is later confined to the Helvetii, these written documents are even rarer. This is not the case for Late La Tène, thanks to the efforts of several authors: Posidonius travelled through Celtic territories at the beginning of the first century BC and certain of his writings are known; Strabo's (63 BC–AD 19) *Geography* gives some information on the tribes settled in the territory of modern Switzerland; Julius Caesar's (100–44 BC) *De Bello Gallico* is informative not only about his campaigns but also about the customs and history of certain Celtic tribes his informers had told him about. It is hardly surprising that there is interesting evidence on the Helvetii of the first century BC. This information will be considered when the events and culture from 450 BC to our era are described.

Chronology

The beginning of the La Tène period is generally dated *c.* 450 BC, though some archaeologists (including E. Vogt) would prefer to date it *c.* 500 BC, stressing the transitory aspect of what was dealt with in Chapter VII as the final Late Hallstatt phase (Ha D2). There are three major divisions of which two are further subdivided. Early La Tène (L T A and B, or B1 and B2; or L T Ia, Ib and Ic) ends *c.* 200 B C, the division between A and B being *c.* 400 B C. Middle La Tène (L T C or II) lasts a little more than two generations, from 200 to 120 B C. Late La Tène (L T D or III) divided into two phases, ends in 58 B C with the onset of the historical period, which in Switzerland involves the great but unsuccessful emigration of the Helvetii and the Roman conquest. This boundary can also be discerned from archaeology in spite of an obvious cultural continuity. L T D1 could be considered an extension of L T C, while L T D2 corresponds to the first stage of the Roman domination of Helvetia and ends at the Christian era.

Fig. 51

THE PLATEAU AND THE JURA

The geographic distinction which we have observed up till now is still justified until the setting up of Roman administration and culture.

Early La Tène (L T A and B)

As already mentioned this period continues without any break other than the introduction of a new style in decorative art, applied mostly to metals. The Celtic migrations which were to come and remake the ethnic map of Switzerland had not yet occurred. There is still discussion about the words of Herodotus, who wrote around the mid-fifth century BC that the flow of the Danube 'starts in the Celtic country near the town

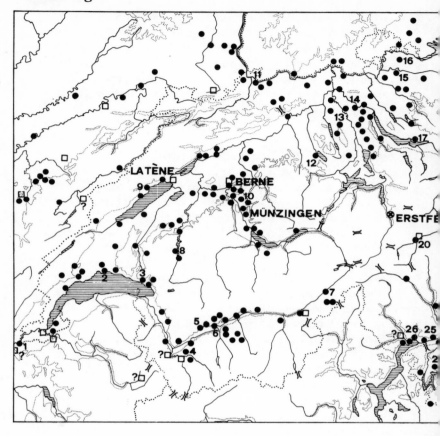

of Pyrene, and cuts Europe in the middle'. Leaving aside the insoluble problem of the allusion to this city which calls to mind the Pyrenean region, this quotation shows us that at the beginning of La Tène south-west Germany, where the sources of the Danube are located, belonged to the Celts. In fact, however, this adds little to our knowledge since it has already been assumed that the Hallstatt groups inhabiting south-west Germany, as well as Switzerland and neighbouring France, were in all probability Celts.

Fig. 51 Early and Middle La Tène. A, *settlement;* B, *cemetery;* C, *Melaun culture (Bronze Age to Late La Tène).*
A,B: 1, *Chancy GE;* 2, *Saint-Sulpice VD;* 3, *Vevey VD;* 4, *Vollège VS, Le Levron;* 5, *Conthey VS;* 6, *Sion VS;* 7, *Ernen VS;* 8, *Marsens FR;* 9, *Bôle NE;* 10, *Stettlen BE;* 11, *Pratteln BL;* 12, *Sursee LU;* 13, *Boswil AG;* 14, *Dietikon ZH;* 15, *Grossandelfingen ZH;* 16, *Basadingen TG;* 17, *Jona SG;* 18, *Oberriet SG, Montlingerberg;* 19, *Coire-Chur GR;* 20, *Trun GR, Darvella;* 21, *Mesocco GR;* 22, *Castaneda GR;* 23, *Arbedo TI, Castione, Cerinesca, Molinazzo, etc.;* 24, *Giubiasco TI;* 25, *Gudo TI;* 26, *Locarno TI, Solduno;* 27, *Cademario.*
C: a, *Koblach AU;* b, *Eschen FL;* c, *Mels SG, Castels;* d, *Tamins GR;* e, *Cazis GR, Cresta;* f, *Süsch GR, Padnal;* g, *Ramosch GR, Mottata.*
Thin dotted line: 700 m altitude

At the end of the fifth century BC migrating groups approached the Alps and crossed them, reaching the north Italian plains from 400 BC onwards, before arriving at Rome in 387–386 BC. It is impossible to prove whether these movements affected Switzerland, but it is difficult to assume that the migratory tribes would have avoided the Plateau. Some migrants may conceivably have at least travelled through the lake Geneva regions and the Rhône to cross the Great Saint-Bernard pass, and perhaps that of Simplon. Among the tribes that had come to settle in the Italian peninsula (Insubri, Boii, Senoni, Lingones, etc.) the Lepontii, whom we shall meet again in the southern Alps, may be mentioned. Their name appears rather late. In any case, archaeology in Switzerland does not provide definite traces of these migratory movements.

Cemeteries   From an archaeological point of view much the same situation applies in Early La Tène as in Early Hallstatt (Ha C): only burials and their contents are available for study and almost nothing is known of the dwellings and settlements of the period. However, a very modest hut can be mentioned whose floor was uncovered at Gelterkinden (Sissach BL); judging from its dimensions (3.60×2.20 m) and its primitive aspect, it must have belonged to a poor farmer.

It is interesting to note that the Late Hallstatt (Ha D) fortified sites have been abandoned, although there are no signs that battles were fought over them. The Wittnauer Horn (Wittnau BL) enclosure was not even completed. It is only in the late Roman period that soldiers take any interest in the hillfort again. Burgenrain (Sissach BL) was also abandoned and only came to life again during the early Middle Ages.

It is even more significant to note that, on the evidence of the burials, there is no break in cultural evolution. The rite of cremation is no longer practised. Inhumation is still customary, quite often under barrows, and most frequently in previously used barrows. But increasingly there are cemeteries with flat tombs in the earth, with the body sometimes surrounded by rounded stones or in a coffin, and usually orientated in a north-south direction. The body is laid out on its back, with the head sometimes resting on a stone. In more than one case a pile of ashes has been deposited above or around the body. Viollier thought the ashes came from the domestic hearth; this custom seems to have been mainly for children. Moreover, in every cemetery the presence of one or several hearths was noted and they doubtless had a funerary function. In the absence of any other evidence, one can deduce from the fact that the tombs never cut across each other that they must have been conspicuous at ground level.

Some of these cemeteries lasted a long time and their extension can be followed through several phases. Thus at Münsingen BE, where over 170 have been counted, people were buried up to the beginning of Middle La Tène around 200 BC. This is also the case with the eighty-five or so tombs at Saint-Sulpice VD, among which only six out of the sixty-two datable tombs date to La Tène A, the others being divided between LT B and B2. At Vevey VD the grave-goods overlap at the end of LT B2 and LT C.

Celts of both sexes were fond of personal ornaments. This, combined with the custom of burial with personal goods, helps the archaeologist who can work on plentiful if not varied material. Men were accompanied by their sheathed iron swords and spears, very rarely by knives or axes. Male ornaments are relatively simple: one or sometimes two bracelets, with a ring in exceptional cases. The predominant ornament is the fibula, made of iron and more rarely of bronze; men sometimes wore three of them and they were obviously used to fasten clothing.

A woman would have in her tomb the ornaments she had worn while alive. Fibulae are more numerous than in small burials and it can be assumed that these brooches were a symbol of wealth. There are two striking examples which demonstrate this fact. At Boswil AG a little girl had twenty-three fibulae in her tomb and at Dietikon ZH a young woman wore fourteen fibulae on her chest. The other jewellery of this last tomb is characteristic: round the neck was a thin bronze chain with a jet bead, on the left elbow a solid bronze bangle, on each wrist and ankle a tubular bangle and, finally, on the right hand, three rings, one made of bronze wire, the other two of silver. In addition, there is the torque which was to become a male ornament at the end of La Tène.

Plate 67

These different elements revealed by the grave-goods may quickly be described and their evolution traced up to *c*. 200 BC.

Weapons   The Early La Tène iron sword is long with a symmetrical double cutting edge and tapering point. The hilt was probably made of wood. It is protected by a scabbard of iron or occasionally of bronze, terminating in a shape which is often perforated and heart-shaped. It is fixed to the belt by two rings and a thong. We will deal later with the skill of the weapon-makers of Middle and Late La Tène; now it must suffice to say that it had already reached a high level as is testified by the engraved decoration on the upper end of a Münsingen BE sword. A spear is also placed on the right side of the warrior beside the sword. It varies from 1·75 to 2·05 m in length. An iron butt reinforces the foot of the shaft and the socketed blade is very elongated. Bow and arrows are absent in

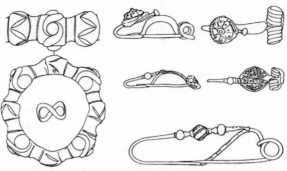

Fig. 52 Early La Tène (LT B2); Münsingen BE, grave 149; bracelet, finger-ring and fibulae. Longest fibula c. 11 cm

the weaponry of this period in Switzerland. The warrior was poorly protected. He wore no helmet and no trace of a shield has ever been found; would it have been made entirely of wood or leather?

Fig. 52

Plate 64

Ornaments The fibula combined the roles of clothes-fastener and jewellery. It varied according to fashion, which makes it useful for chronological classification. Without entering into details, its principal characteristics may be described. The fibula was made of iron or bronze. It lost the sometimes odd characteristics of certain Hallstatt fibulae and became more regular, with a bow which at first was slight but then became wider. The spring is usually symmetrical with two whorls on either end joined by an outer cord. The catch is made longer and very soon is decorated with a knob and is turned back towards the bow, thereby adding to the decoration. Indeed, the bow, which is at first simply decorated with engravings and reliefs, becomes very sophisticated with diversified motifs in which the spiral plays a great part; coral or a substitute of red enamel are often used as well as bone.

Torques are closed or open and are decorated with bosses and complicated mouldings. They are also finished with coral and enamel. Bracelets and anklets are rather diversified, being closed or open with a varying amount of decoration. At the end of the period bracelets with fluting and large bosses are manufactured.

Rings are scarce at the beginning of La Tène but now diversify. They are made of bronze, silver or gold, and are thread-like or ring-shaped.

Bent, thread-like saddle-shaped rings found at the end of Early La Tène may be mentioned. Among the remaining ornaments are rare pendants or beads made of blue glass, as well as glass rings of various shades which foreshadow the birth of a proper glass industry in Middle La Tène. The part which the Mediterranean area played in the development of this technique is symbolized by the presence in Saint-Sulpice VD tomb 22 (LT B2) of two polychrome glass pendants depicting two bearded human heads with foreheads covered with curly hair; their Punic origin is clearly illustrated and provides an interesting glimpse of Transalpine or Rhône trade.

Plate 66

Amber was still in demand. It was used for rings or large beads. A child burial at Münsingen BE had a necklace of 142 amber beads, some of which were as large as a walnut. Only systematic research with physico-chemical methods could determine whether the amber came from the Baltic or from Sicily. Lignite and jet were used to make pendant-rings; the manufacture of bracelets had almost entirely ceased.

An examination of the distribution map of Early La Tène ornaments makes it possible to establish an evolution of taste through succeeding generations on the one hand, and variations according to the regions of the Plateau on the other. Thus, fibulae richly decorated with enamel and coral are particularly plentiful in the Münsingen BE cemetery as well as in the whole Bernese area. Torques become rarer during this period. This feminine ornament first begins to be less popular in the Berne regions (LT B1) and then in western Switzerland (LT B2), while the Celts in north-east Switzerland retain it longer. The same applies to the use of bronze or iron bracelets. The bent thread-like bracelets are plentiful except in western Switzerland. Unfortunately, it is impossible to know whether the differences correspond to tribal diversities. This hypothesis should not be excluded however.

From the study of Early La Tène burials, and of the material they contained, the impression emerges of a quite dense, prosperous and peaceful population in which craftsmen – bronze and iron metal-workers, jewellers, etc. – were masters of technique.

Middle and Late La Tène (LT C and D)

History Calm seems to have reigned over Switzerland in the northern Alps for half a century. This can be inferred from the continued use of several cemeteries on the Plateau such as Andelfingen ZH, Münsingen BE and to a lesser degree Vevey (*Viviscus*) VD. This impression is supported by the fact that both large and small cemeteries were created, around Berne for example, which seems to indicate that occupation density was increasing. This relative quiet corresponding to silence in ancient authors' writings was to be upset by the repercussions of migrations of a northern origin. The Germanic peoples still exerted an increasing pressure on the Celtic tribes. Among these the Helvetii, located in south-west Germany, had probably begun sending small groups to be settled across the Rhine in the Aar valley and thus on the territory which was supposed to belong to the Sequani. This time, i.e. in 113 BC, they clashed with the Cimbrians who were on warlike migrations.

It is not easy to relate in a few words a coherent tale of the events during the following years, but the essential points can be noted. We know that the Helvetii left their territory, leaving behind them what was later called 'the desert of the Helvetii' by Greek and Roman writers. As they proceeded through the area between the Rhine, the Jura and the Alpine foothills, the Cimbrians drew two Helvetian groups, the Teutoni and the Tigurini, into the famous expedition of 109 BC, which took them through Provence to Aquitaine amid looting and destruction. There, on the Garonne not far from Agen, the Tigurini in 107 BC defeated the army of the Roman consul Lucius Cassius Longinus who was killed. After a detour along the Atlantic coast the Tigurini, led by the valiant young chief Divico, joined the Cimbrians and the Teutoni in a raid along the Rhône valley. They defeated two Roman armies at Orange then parted to resume their migration. The Tigurini were fortunate or wise enough to leave this warlike association, avoiding the fate of the Cimbrians and Teutoni who were annihilated by Marius in battles at Aix-en-Provence in 102 BC and at Vercelli in northern Italy in 101 BC. Having migrated towards Norique, the Tigurini, persuaded by Sylla, joined the main body of the Helvetii and settled in the Aventicum region, the future capital of Roman Helvetia.

From this much condensed history it should be remembered that some of the Helvetii from the end of the second century BC had on the one hand come to know south-west Gaul with its good climate and natural resources, and on the other had victoriously fought the Roman armies. In addition Rome, not long before (*c.* 120 BC), had conquered the territory between the Mediterranean, the Rhône, lake Geneva and the foot of the Alps where the Vocontii and the Allobrogi lived. Just beyond lake Geneva, the Allobrogi town of Genua (Geneva) constituted the most advanced garrison in the direction of the Helvetii and the Sequani, whom they had repulsed across the Jura.

The oppida   For half a century nothing significant happened. One can speculate that the Helvetii, free from the pressure of the Germani, lived quite peacefully on the new lands. However, it was probably not completely quiet as fortified positions were created throughout this period: at first these were mere shelters doubling the rural agglomer-ations; later they became real oppida. They have not all been excavated systematically but the best-known example is the one on the Enge peninsula which is formed by a meander of the Aar as it leaves Berne. Here, the entrance was barred by a simple ditch. But at Berne-Tiefenau dwellings were located outside the shelter. The situation is slightly different at Geneva which had been under Roman domination since 120 BC. Here the oppidum, dominating the Rhône where it flows out of the lake towards the land of the Helvetii and Sequani, does not seem to have been occupied before the forced return of the Helvetii after their attempted emigration in 58 BC.

The site of La Tène   As the type site of the second phase of the Iron Age, La Tène deserves further mention; the interpretation of the site still gives rise to discussion. There is nothing left to be seen at the site, which is situated on the former river bed of the Thièle (Zihl) where it flows out from lake Neuchâtel (Marin-Epagnier NE commune). This site has been known since 1858 and excavations were started in 1874 after the lowering of the lake-level (correction of the Jura waters); work continued until 1885, and resumed again between 1907 and 1917. The main observations can be summarized as follows: there were two carefully built bridges and between them a complex of piles and beams, not easily discernible. There may have been constructions on the southern bank while the northern bank was probably reinforced by fences.

The importance of La Tène lies in its wealth of objects as well as in their variety and quality. For example, there were over 150 swords –

Plate 70

many still in their scabbards – nearly 270 spearheads – 5 with their shafts – 22 shield-umbos (shield-bosses) and 7 more or less complete shields, 385 fibulae, over 50 phalerae, numerous tools, wooden objects, including a wheel and a yoke, not to mention coins. Pottery is represented to a small extent. All this material attests the occupation of the site during the whole of La Tène C (II) and a little later. Thus it lasted about one century.

The first problem posed by La Tène is its interpretation. The first question concerns the double bridge, whose use is obvious: it made passage possible to the centre of the Swiss Plateau (more precisely the Berne region which, as we know, was heavily colonized) and to the Jura whose cross-valleys led to eastern Gaul. It seems clear that many of the objects gathered in the bed of the Thièle – tools, harness-pieces – can best be explained by the presence of a permanent observation post. P. Vouga, who wrote the final report on the site (1923), rejected the idea of a toll-post put forward by J. Déchelette and proposed that it was 'a fortified warehouse, militarily occupied'. The exclusively Celtic character of the material, the absence of 'evidence of family occupation', the great scarcity of objects belonging to women, the abundance of weapons, the presence of repair workshops and not those of manufacture: all these arguments proceed in the same direction. To justify such an hypothesis, there is no need to imagine that the Thièle was a tribal boundary, possibly between the Sequani and the Helvetii.

More recently Raddatz has expressed another opinion, based on evidence from northern Europe. He proposes that at La Tène there is a sanctuary where objects could have been dedicated to the water deity. This would explain the presence of these objects in the earlier bed of the Thièle on the one hand, and that of several skeletons on the other, some of which bear traces of unhealed sword wounds on the skull.

Fig. 53

The discovery by Mlle H. Schwab in 1965–66 of another bridge on the Thièle, at Cornaux NE, two miles downstream, raised the question again. Indeed, in the mud, mixed in with the debris of the bridge which had obviously collapsed, there were a certain number of objects, including weapons, tools, and pottery, and in particular several more or less complete skeletons: several of the skulls had been broken. M. R. Müller, a specialized engineer, examined the hydrographical and sedimentological conditions and came to the conclusion that this bridge

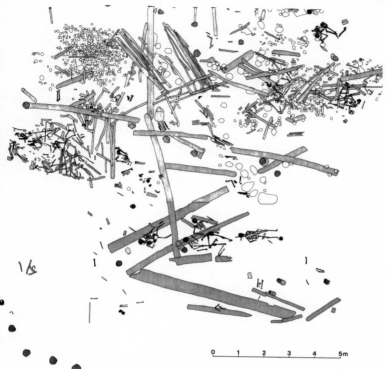

Fig. 53 Middle La Tène; Cornaux NE; collapsed bridge in the river Thièle, with skeletons of wounded men and women (in black); wooden piles and beams are shaded; the northern shore-line is indicated by gravel. Courtesy Miss H. Schwab, ACF

and the people on it had succumbed to a sudden flood originating on lake Neuchâtel. This seems to require us to attribute the destruction of the La Tène post to the same natural cause. Thus it is not necessary to find a politico-military event to explain the sudden break in activity at this important post. In any case, there does not seem to be a paradox between the two principal hypotheses put forward: a military post and a sanctuary devoted to a local divinity might have existed at the same place.

The late D. F. Allen, who had recently resumed the study of coins found at La Tène and in the vicinity, made the following observations. A local mint would have existed; moreover, 'the regular Celtic gold coinage found belongs to a single phase, late in the second or early in the first century BC'; the silver and potin coinage probably stop around 70–65 BC; this tends to give a later date to the destruction of the site. Study of the geographic and tribal origin of imported coins at La Tène reveals that most came from the west and south. Most would be of the Sequani and, more rarely, of the Aedui; gold coins, on the other hand, are of Helvetian type. Finally, the presence of more recent coinage indicates a slight occupation of no real significance after the destruction of the site and, more precisely, after the return of the Helvetii.

Burials　There is no important change in funerary rites. Flat tombs with the bodies lying on their backs are still used. Investigations at Vevey VD have shown the use of wooden coffins, whose lower part was cut from a tree-trunk; no nails were used to make the lid. The obolos funerary rite (a coin in the mouth to pay for passage to the after-life) was observed in certain places.

Social and economic divisions　The significant disparities in grave-goods in the same cemetery make it possible to establish two facts. On the one hand, they indicate a certain democratic equality in death, since the most wealthy and powerful are not inhumed separately; on the other hand, they show the existence of economic classes which probably correspond to social classes. What is known from ancient texts and Celtic legends confirms the latter hypothesis, but till now archaeology has been unable to give evidence of princely burials which had existed elsewhere in the Celtic world. Equality in death corresponds well to the assembly of free men which was sovereign to a certain extent. This social situation declined during the first century, with the patrician families tending to keep power to themselves.

Material culture　Continuity is clearly evident in the material of Early La Tène as well as during the following phases, so that we will only point out differences of particular interest.

Weapons　The sword is longer, up to 1 m (LT D1), with a more blunted point, and the profile of the hilt-guard is higher. It often becomes a masterpiece with complicated techniques applied to iron: welding of thin juxtaposed plates, granulating, stamping, use of acid with reserved waxed areas. The blade often bears a stamp-mark near the hilt. On one issued from Port (Nidau BE) the stamp – depicting the tree of life between two ibexes – appears with a name in Greek: KOPICIOC (Korisios). It may be recalled, if Caesar is to be believed, that the Romans would have found in the camp of the Helvetii, who were defeated at Bibracte in 58 BC, tablets written in Greek bearing a census of migrant tribes. Some of the swords from the sites of La Tène and Port are decorated with motifs in which the style of the period, derived from plant and animal themes, is elegantly expressed.

Plate 68

Plate 76

Towards the end of Middle La Tène, the 'anthropoid daggers' appear with a hilt imitating a human body with outstretched limbs, the head being only a boss. They evolve in the anthropomorphization of the head. The hypothesis has been put forward that daggers of this type, which are widespread in Switzerland, were made there; perhaps they were the product of a specialized workshop.

In Middle La Tène spear-points are surprisingly varied. One from the bed of the Thièle bears on either side a beautiful asymmetrical motif. There are arrowheads; a fragment of a yew bow found at the site of La Tène testifies to their use. There is, however, no real evidence of the use of the sling, although Caesar observed it among the Gauls. Shields are now well known to us, including three quite complete examples from La Tène itself, made of wood strengthened by an iron umbo (centre boss). The coat of mail is attested by small fragments. Only one example of a helmet is known on the Plateau. It was found at Port (Nidau BE), a site similar to La Tène. The helmet was probably the attribute of a nobleman, to whom also was reserved the use of horses and therefore of spurs. The use of war-chariots can be deduced from the presence of wheel and harness elements at La Tène and Berne-Tiefenau.

Plate 77

Personal ornaments The fibula is still popular. It is generally made of bronze and consists of a catch joined to the bow by a clip. With a few exceptions decoration grows poorer. In LT D the fibula is elongated and becomes thinner; it is sometimes cast in a mould though it retains its shape. There is also a cross-bow fibula with transverse spring. The torque disappears as a female ornament. Metal bracelets are progressively replaced as early as Middle La Tène by glass bracelets, which offer in the course of time a fairly large variety of forms, colours and decoration. Rings made of bronze, electrum, silver and gold are more frequent, especially those of spiral wire and those with a stone. The belt made of a

Plate 74, *Fig. 54*

Plate 72

Plate 71

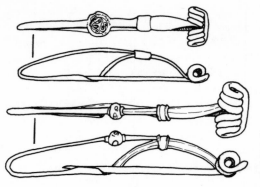

Fig. 54 Middle La Tène (LT C); Münsingen BE; fibulae. Max. length c. 10.5 cm

metal chain, hitherto extremely rare, becomes more popular from Middle La Tène; it was reserved for women.

Tools, crafts and art Thanks mainly to the discoveries from the site of La Tène, we have valuable and informative evidence of the tools used by the craftsmen of this period. The skill of the metalworker who made beautiful swords has already been mentioned. He also manufactured tools used by other craftsmen: bronze and woodworkers (saws, files, nails, wheel rims, etc.), and leather workers, including a leather case containing small instruments certainly used by saddle makers. The ability of the metalworkers allowed them to produce some interesting works of decorative art. The most remarkable is the Port bronze ring on to which bull heads and birds are welded.

Plate 73

Coinage We have already mentioned that there was probably a mint at La Tène. It followed the tradition of the Celtic coin makers who used to imitate and adapt Greek models. Minting began in the second century BC, using as a model for the coins the gold stater of Philip II of Macedonia. Switzerland appears to have been a centre for producing gold coins, thanks to the productivity of the rivers in the centre of the Plateau. Posidonius notes their exploitation in the beginning of the first century BC. It is possible to make out the presence of a workshop in the north east of the country, with a coin distribution limited to this area (AG, ZH, TG, LU) during the La Tène C (Unterentfelden AG type). Another type, 'Regenbogenschüsselchen', more degenerate but imitating the same model, is attributed to the Boii and is well known in Switzerland.

The great migration

Our purpose is not to relate in detail the story of the abortive migration of the Helvetii in 58 BC, but a few words are necessary as it is part of the tradition of the Celtic migrations, of which one, less than two generations before, led the Helvetii to the Swiss Plateau and the Jura. That migration resulted in the loss of their independence and their submission to Rome.

Caesar, in spite of some inaccuracies, remains a remarkable documentary source. What he says about the Helvetii before 58 BC allows us to picture quite well this people who planned their departure carefully and at length, full of memories of their last migrations and harassed again by the Germani. It is of little interest, from our point of view, to know how this great project was combined with the ambitions of Orgetorix, a patrician who, accused of wishing to become king, chose suicide instead of torture by fire.

It is noteworthy that the Helvetii decided not to proceed towards Italy, the traditional destination of so many Celtic tribes, but towards south-west Gaul which the oldest among them – for instance Divico who was then a young chief – had known half a century earlier and of which they kept glorious memories. It is also interesting to note the determination and method, which does not usually conform to the Celtic character, with which the journey was organized. A census was made; it was decided to carry out a scorched earth policy in order to delay those who would occupy the abandoned territory: Caesar speaks of about 12 towns and 400 villages which were burnt. He estimates that the total number of migrating Helvetii was 263,000 souls, to which must be added 105,000 allies, Rauraci and Boiensi, drawn into the adventure. These numbers, published when Caesar was anxious to make his victory greater, must be read with great caution. In any case, the sheer number of people, men, women and children involved, with overloaded chariots and cattle, made the enterprise hazardous.

To leave their territory the easiest route open to the Helvetii led past a strip of land between lake Geneva and the Jura, then through Geneva and the Rhône valley. To go this way meant they had to cross part of the territory of the Allobrogi who were still under Roman domination. The result is well known: Caesar, warned of the Helvetian plan – though they came with no warlike intentions – rushed to the area with his troops, fortified in haste the weak sectors of the Allobrogi bank of the Rhône and removed the flooring of the bridge over the river. He delayed negotiations with the chiefs of the Helvetii, including Divico, until he was sure of his position, and then forbade the crossing. When the Helvetii resigned themselves to the difficult task of passing between the Jura and Mont Vuache by the right bank of the Rhône, he met them on the Saône. Here he defeated the Tigurini, and then forced back the rest of the migrating population to the north before crushing them at Bibracte, one of the Edueni oppida near Autun, Saône-et-Loire.

Vanquished and reduced in number, the Helvetii bowed to their conqueror and returned to their lands. The Allobrogi had to supply them with wheat so that their return should not end in famine. Caesar had in mind an even greater enterprise: the Gallic Wars had begun.

Archaeology has revealed only a few traces of this history. No burnt layer has been recognized corresponding to the destruction of settlements by the Helvetii and the Rauraci. But a small part of Caesar's defensive system (the *murus*) along the terraces overlooking the Rhône at Avully GE have been found as well as some beams of the northern abutment of the Celtic bridge at Geneva.

Archaeology does, however, provide evidence of the reconstruction of towns and villages by the Helvetii who had returned home and were under Roman domination. These are mostly oppida where the population lived permanently. The most important are: the Enge peninsula oppidum at Berne, fortified with a wall, the famous *murus gallicus* made of earth strengthened by external and internal beams. Mont Vully FR, between lakes Neuchâtel and Morat, might have preceded Aventicum (Avenches VD) as capital of the Helvetii. There is the double loop of the Rhine at Rheinau ZH downstream from Schaffhausen and on German territory at Altenburg, each barred by a *vallum*. On the Rauraci territory, at the elbow of the Rhine on the left bank, there are the two Basle fortified sites, one near the old gas factory at the bottom, the other, the Cathedral hill. It is also worth mentioning the potters' village in the bottom of the valley at Brühl (Sissach BL). Among the localities testified by La Tène finds – and whose names often derive from Celtic names – we may mention Nyon VD (*Noviodunum*), Lausanne VD (*Leusonna*), Yverdon VD (*Eburodunum*), Windisch AG (*Vindonissa*). Others at this period are known only by their names:

Fig. 55

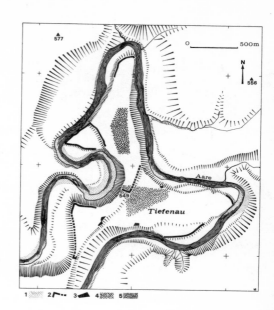

Fig. 55 Middle and Late La Tène; Berne, Engehalbinsel and Tiefenau; site of the settlements before (4) and after (5) the migration of 58 BC. 1, modified banks of the Aar river; 2, walls; 3, cemeteries

Minnodunum (Moudon VD), *Salodurum* (Soleure), *Tenedo* (Zurzach ZH), *Vitudurum* (Winterthour ZH), etc.

A very important fact established by archaeology is the continuity in material culture despite the migration of 58 BC. Certainly there is a distinct phase of La Tène D2 after that date, but the differences are not marked. Pottery is much better known thanks to the dwelling sites. There are clearly specialized workshops, like that of Sissach-Brühl BL, which distributed their products. The potter's wheel was introduced from the south along with certain shapes, for instance the narrow-footed jar. Decoration is made by stamping, burnishing or painting. The polychrome painted vessels with geometric motifs or motifs inspired by animals or plants lasted quite a long time, even into the first century AD.

At the very beginning of the reoccupation of their territory the Helvetii, who were considered as confederates (*foederati*) of Rome, were placed only under the conqueror's civilian administration. This can be seen in the weak network of garrisons. But from 50 BC onwards, probably after some unsuccessful rebellions by the Helvetii, Rome tightened its control: about 50 BC, Caesar founded the *Colonia equestris* centred on Nyon VD with the help of his cavalry veterans; by doing so,

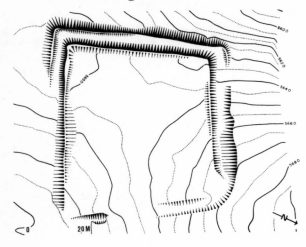

Fig. 56 Late La Tène; Bremgartnerwald near Berne; square sanctuary (Viereckschanze)

he made sure that the episode of 58 BC would not be repeated. About the same time L. Munatius Plancus, conqueror of the Reti, established the *Colonia Rauracorum* to the east of Basle (which was to become the great *Augusta Raurica*) in order to protect the line of the Rhine where the Germani constituted a permanent threat.

Fig. 56

The Helvetii, though under Roman domination, continued their traditional way of life, including their religion. Archaeologists have not found much physical evidence for the latter except for the square sanctuaries uncovered at Ramsen SH and at Berne which belong to the group of these religious structures whose centre is in southern Germany. Like many other aspects of religion, the sanctuaries survived the Roman period by becoming stone buildings, as at Petinesca, Studen BE.

It was not until the reign of Augustus that increasing Roman domination was accompanied by the acculturation of the Helvetii. This process took longer in the mountainous regions.

THE ALPS

The western Alps
Texts and inscriptions tell us the names of the tribes populating the Valais by the middle of the first century BC. Following the Rhône from

lake Geneva there are the Nantuates (this name has the same meaning as that of the present Valais inhabitants: people from the 'nant', or from the valley) whose chief town was probably Massongex VS (*Tarnaiae*) or Saint-Maurice VS (*Acaunum*); the Veragri, centred on *Octodurus* (Martigny VS); the Seduni (*Sedunum*, Sion VS); and finally the Uberi, probably from Brigue VS (*Briga*). In 57 BC these groups successfully resisted an attempted conquest by Caesar's lieutenant, S. Supicius Galba. It was only in 25 BC that the Romans occupied the Great Saint-Bernard Transalpine route (*Mons Poeninus*), controlled at the Rhône by the city of *Octodurus* (Martigny VS). Between 15 BC and 10 BC Augustus conquered the entire Valais.

It is easy to understand that the Celtic tradition should persist longer in the Valais than on the Plateau. Unfortunately archaeological evidence for the whole period of La Tène is still very fragmentary. What there is comes mostly from burials and shows links between the culture of the Valais and that of the Plateau, though there were quite strong influences from northern Italy and from the Tessin. The crossing of the Great Saint-Bernard pass is attested by many Celtic coins from many areas, thrown by travellers as offerings to the local divinity whom Jupiter Poeninus succeeded. No systematic investigations have yet been made in the Simplon. Passes which appear less accessible at first glance had probably been used, as was the Théodule pass above Zermatt and the one at Albrun which leads to the Binn valley (where a Celtic community lived) and to the Ossola valley and the lake Maggiore region. The passes have been emphasized here because they probably

Plate 75

Fig. 57

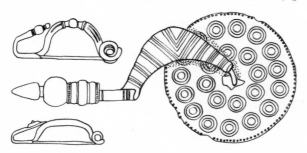

Fig. 57 Early La Tène in the Alps; Loëche-les-Bains – Leukerbad VS; fibulae and fibula with disc. Length of shortest fibula c. 6.7 cm

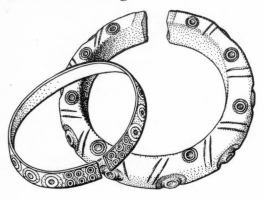

Fig. 58 Late La Tène in the Alps; Valais; bronze bracelets valaisans of two types. Left: flat type (Uberi ?); right: thick type (Veragri ?). Inner diameters c. 7 cm

played a great part in the lives of the population on both sides of the mountain range, by allowing them to take advantage of economic exploitation in both transport and toll.

Fig. 58

Among the finds at La Tène which are specific to the Valais, bronze bracelets occupy a distinctive place. They are characterized by concentric circles, often deeply engraved. There are three types: the first two are open and more or less flat and could be attributed to the Seduni and the Uberi, whereas the third, which is solid and generally closed, could belong to the Veragri; it lasted till about the middle of the first century AD.

The Erstfeld hoard

Plate 78

In the central region of the Alps there is only one interesting find. It was uncovered in 1962 near Erstfeld UR in the upper valley of the Reuss during work undertaken to protect a road against avalanches, on the way which led, from the thirteenth century AD onwards, to the Saint-Gothard pass and to the Tessin. There under a rock were four necklaces and three bracelets, hollow, all of gold and brand-new. They were certainly issued from a single workshop and some were made by the same jeweller. Though they are all related to the Celtic art of Early La Tène they show two sources of inspiration: the necklaces with their mixed and distorted animal and human themes point to the Asian steppes, whereas the plant motifs of the bracelets indicate Italy and Greece.

It is impossible to explain here the presence of this hoard in what was probably a dead-end by the second half of the fourth century BC.

Leaving aside great artistic value, this find demonstrates the interest the Celts had in the Alps.

The territory of the Reti

Together with the southern Tyrol, the Grisons were the country of the Reti to whom Polybius referred in the second century BC. They lived on the Italian side and in the Upper Rhine region up to lake Constance. After having distinguished themselves by raids into the territories of the Helvetii, Rauraci and Sequani, they were conquered by Augustus in 15 BC in a hard campaign. What was their ethnic and linguistic status? This question is still discussed. They may have spoken an Indo-European language with Etruscan affinities. But it is highly probable that some communities under the name of Reti lived closely mingled with Celtic groups, including the Leponti from the Tessin.

This Celtic influence is illustrated in the material culture of La Tène which shows distinctive traits as does the Tyrolian pottery from Fritzen-Sanzeno with fine beakers, and the Schneller beaker (from the eponymous site at Eschnerberg FL) with impressed and incised decoration.

Fig. 59

Imports from the south, brought mainly through the Lukmanier TI-GR and the Uomo TI passes and especially through the San Bernardino GR pass, are not surprising since they prove the persistence of the already well-established trade routes and an ethnic community on either side of the Alps. In the Grisons there are serpentiform fibulae from the Tessin

Plate 81

Fig. 59 Early La Tène in the Alps; Grisons – Graubünden and Liechtenstein; pottery. Left: Fläsch GR, Luzisteig; centre and right: Eschen FL, Schneller. Max. ht. c. 15 cm

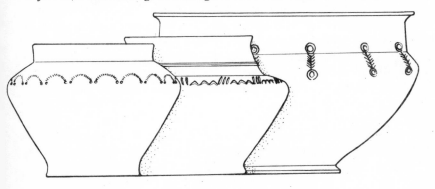

(Golasecca culture). There is also the more spectacular Raschlinas (Präz GR) slab which bears a short funerary inscription in Lepontic characters, as well as the helmet found in the Grisons, no one knows exactly where, which is of Etruscan type. A similar helmet occurs on a bronze statuette depicting a divine or human warrior found with other statuettes at the foot of what was probably a sanctuary on the rocky hill of Gutenberg (Balzers FL). G. von Merhart has written: 'the Gutenberg Mars appears in all its features as the Retic translation of the old Greek or Etruscan design'. The presence of a wild boar beside male and androgynous human figures takes us back to the Celtic world.

The presence of Celts settled on the territory of the Reti is testified by the Darvella (Truns⁄Trun GR) excavations on the lower Rhine, 850 m in altitude, on the road which leads to the Lukmanier pass and perhaps also to Oberalp and Furka, i.e. towards the Valais. Here there are dwellings associated with tombs rich in objects which make it possible to date them to two phases of La Tène (LT B2 and C). Though a great number of these objects are of southern Alpine origin, the majority (swords, fibulae), as well as the pottery found in the houses, are linked to the Celtic world.

There is much more information on dwellings in the area of the Reti than in the Plateau and the Valais. Several house foundations were explored on hills overlooking the valleys. In lower Engadine GR there is Muotto del Clüs (Zernez), Padnal (Süs), Scuol⁄Schuls, Mottata⁄on⁄Ramosch; in the lower Rhine valley there is Darvella (Truns⁄Trun), Grepault (Ringgenberg), and a little further downstream from the lower Rhine valley there are several sites, the most important of which is situated on the great 'Inselberg' of Montlingerberg SG. Dwellings are made of dry⁄stone foundations with vertical posts supporting the walls and roof. At Coire (Chur GR) one La Tène level has produced objects from the region of the Golasecca culture mixed with other indigenous and Celtic material. Some have considered Coire to be a market situated at this crossroads. We have omitted the Grisons valleys which face south since they belong to the domain of the Tessin and northern Italy.

Plate 79

The Italian side of the Alps

The fine culture we have seen developing in the Tessin during the first half of the first millennium BC continues to evolve, thanks to its own vitality and above all to the influences it received from people of the Italian peninsula, especially from the Etruscans, then from Celtic invaders after 400 BC, and finally from the Romans who were in full expansion from the end of the third century BC. Here it may briefly be recalled that around 390 BC the Celts, filtering through several Alpine passes, spread in several waves across northern Italy where some of their groups settled. The Romans, proceeding by degrees to the same plain of the Po then to the central Alps, gained a decisive advantage by occupying Milan (*Mediolanum*) in 222 BC. Their defeat in 218 BC on the Tessin and the Trebbia while opposing Hannibal's army only delayed them a little in their stubborn conquest. In 196 BC the taking of Come (*Comum*) was followed by the submission of the Insubri. In 183 BC, the Senate informed the cis-Alpine Gauls that its domination reached the Alps.

In fact this announcement was somewhat hypothetical for the territory nearest to the foot of the Alps. The Leponti tribe lived there, Celtic but certainly crossed with the natives who spoke another Indo-European dialect. Whereas their cousins to the north of the Alps were writing in Greek or Latin characters, they borrowed their alphabet from the Etruscans. This is known from about 100 inscriptions in the Tessin, in the Mesolcina GR valley and in neighbouring regions, including Raschlinas, Präz GR, already mentioned.

Plate 84

The inhabitants of the Leponti country played the same role as those of the Valais. They organized the Transalpine trade and their monopoly assured them relative economic prosperity. The pass across San Bernardino (1607 m) went along the Mesolcina valley where two sites directly involved in this traffic have been explored: Castaneda and Mesocco (Misox GR); the latter is associated with a wall which bars the road (a toll-gate?).

The arrival of the Celts did not deeply alter the indigenous way of life, except probably in the social field, as the impression is given that the relatively few newcomers constituted a ruling class. In any case, the large cemeteries, and thus the corresponding settlements, kept spreading without a gap in continuity, as for instance those of Giubiasco TI with over five hundred tombs, and those of Cerinasca (Arbedo TI). Other cemeteries began after 400 BC. These were still in use after the introduction of Roman culture.

Plate 83
Plate 85

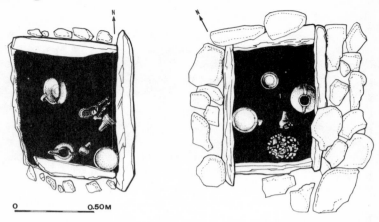

Fig. 60 Early La Tène south of the Alps (LT B, Golasecca III); Pazzallo TI; cremation cists with grave-goods. Left: grave 1 (oenochoë and largest fibula, see next fig.); right: grave 2

Fig. 61 Pazzallo TI; grave 1 (see fig. 60). Left: large fibula sanguisuga, *alone (left) and with attached ornaments; right: oenochoë*

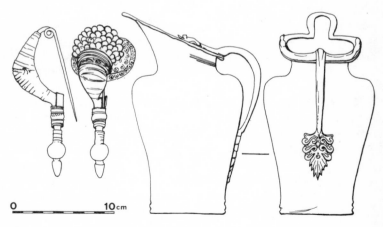

The traditional funerary rites persisted with the coexistence of cremation and inhumation. Grave-goods show the cultural mixing; the indigenous objects relating to the Golasecca culture appear side by side with Celtic La Tène material. In this connection it is interesting to note that the Celtic swords of the Tessin belong to types from Gaul which are unknown in Switzerland.

Plate 87
Figs. 60, 61

The threat followed by the domination of Rome after 200 BC does not seem to have altered the cultural life of the Leponti to any great extent. The appearance of helmets in some tombs and of a greater quantity of bronze vessels has already been noted; they testify to the intensification of commercial links with the south. In addition, the population of the Tessin probably kept a relative independence.

The settlement of this region during the second phase of the Iron Age is known only from the villages of Castaneda and Mesocco-Misox GR. They probably looked like traditional Tessin hamlets, made up of small

Fig. 62 Early La Tène south of the Alps; Castaneda GR; north Etruscan inscription (alphabet of Sondrio) on the rim of an oenochoë; late 5th century BC. Transcription: 1, PEKEZLSEZT : ASTSTAZ : XVSAS (after Whatmough, 1936 and ASA, 1938); or 2, LEKEZLSEZT : ASTSTAZ : CHVSVS (after Nogara, 1939). Translation (partly hypothetical): 1, Property of Sextus Astustus (or Astusta), son of Beccius (= son of Beccus' son), of Cussa (?); or 2, Sextus Astustus, son of Legius Cussa (or Cussus)

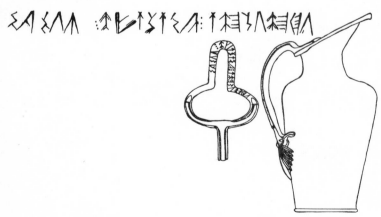

houses with dry-stone walls. At Castaneda they stand close to each other. At both sites the burials have been studied.

Plate 86

Among the objects which attest to the wealth of the inhabitants in the valleys on the Italian side of the Alps are, for the beginning of the period, the bronze oenochoes brought from Etruria or manufactured by imitating those in the Tessin workshops. The most distinctive one was found at Castaneda GR where there were several in the necropolis. It is characterized by an engraved inscription on the rim of the spout in letters of an alphabet which is not of a north Etruscan type. It dates from the end of the fifth century BC. Later, the prosperity of the Leponti is clear in the use of silver for personal ornaments, alongside traditional materials.

Fig. 62

History teaches us that Romans were kept out of the Alpine valleys for nearly a century by the hostility of the inhabitants, jealous of their independence and of their monopoly of the routes and passes. This situation ended only in 15 BC under Augustus, when military operations led to the conquest of the whole Alps and the submission of its population. The valleys of the Tessin and the Grisons to the south of the Alpine range suffered a common fate. In 6 BC Augustus inscribed on to the great trophy of Turbia among the names of the forty-six tribes of the conquered Alps:

. . .LEPONTI · VBERI · NANTVATES · SEDVNI · VARAGRI · SALASSI . . .

That is really the end of prehistory.

CHAPTER X

Conclusions

In concluding this introduction to the pre- and protohistory of Switzerland several questions may be asked. Is it possible to discern any constant trends running through these millennia? If so, for what reasons? In Chapter I we stressed the importance of a relief where the Alps-Plateau-Jura determines the direction of migratory movements and conditions demographic distributions. Has this geographical determinism played the leading part in Swiss prehistory? What is man's role during the various stages of settlement in Switzerland?

Being convinced of the part played by human free will, we will not be taken in by the old determinist trap. Nevertheless, the formula 'Switzerland, turntable of Europe', noted at the beginning of this book, is partially justified for the periods in question. From the Neolithic onwards Switzerland has been a meeting-place. This is particularly true during the Neolithic when cultures converged on the Swiss Plateau from several sources, mostly Central European and Mediterranean. It is the same at the beginning of the Early Bronze Age. From the Middle Bronze Age onwards influences from Germany and Central Europe predominated and currents from the southern Alps were not strong enough to counter-balance them.

During the second phase of the Iron Age (La Tène) the call from the south ('Drang nach Süden') which took hold of the Celts, driven by migratory movements from the north, brought an essential function to the passes of the Alps, and therefore to those of the Swiss Alps, the effects of which were felt in northern Italy.

When the Romans, anxious not to see another invasion like that of the Celts, thought of protecting their expanding empire, geography demanded that Switzerland become one of its borders.

History will only repeat itself. The stubborn strength of the Germanic peoples, who were compelled a few centuries later to follow in the footsteps of the migrating Celts, made a battle-field of Switzerland. Here Rome lost its power to the 'Barbarians', though Romanity retained some of its rights.

Conclusions

Under this influence Burgundians, Alemanni and Franks were transformed. Feudal Switzerland sprang from it, but the major routes of the Plateau and the Alpine passes meant political and religious subservience. During the twelfth century an awakening among the communes of a desire for liberty and wealth gave rise in central Switzerland to the alliance of the Waldstätten, those mountaineers who in 1291 formed the core of what became, after many vicissitudes, the Swiss Confederation.

It is true that geographical factors mark the pre- and protohistory as well as the history of Switzerland, but men and their cultural traits have also actively participated in forging their own destiny. The internal dynamism of cultures and the possibilities of adaptation to new lands certainly played a part, at least after the Neolithic. In this way one can explain the success of the Middle Neolithic cultures, united under the name of the Cortaillod culture; the brilliance of the Early Bronze Age Rhône culture, which although based on attraction to copper sources, surely owed much to the skill of the metalworkers; the importance of human occupations during the Late Bronze Age when the skilled crafts of bronze and pottery existed together with a well-structured social organization, allowing the diffusion of techniques, ideas and people; the power and wealth of the Hallstatt feudal groups who combined the advantages of soil exploitation with those of trade from the south; and the mobility and expansion of the Celts during the La Tène era. One could end by calling to mind the imperialist will of the Romans, overcoming all natural obstacles and human opposition.

The remotest history of Switzerland is not distinctive or unusual; its main interest lies in this interaction between the restraints of the environment and the genius of man. Historians take the place of prehistorians to tell how these forces have led to present Switzerland, which, despite apparently being condemned to isolation in its small territory, is nevertheless open to the whole world.

Sources of Illustrations

The following persons and institutions kindly permitted use to be made of photographs taken or owned by them and their help is gratefully acknowledged.

BHM 2, 5–7, 30, 33, 34, 36, 37, 53–55, 58, 72, 74; DAGR 48; DAUG 13–16, 21, 24, 25, 27; Grau, Zug 38; Gross SG 47; HMSG 46; KASO 61, 63; KMUZG 40; Laboratorium für Urgeschichte, University BS 1; LM 8, 9, 11, 17, 18, 26, 28, 29, 31, 32, 39, 41–43, 45, 49, 52, 59, 60, 64, 67–69, 70 (below), 73, 75, 78, 81–87; MAHF 35, 51, 56, 57; MCAHL 62, 66; MCAN 19, 44, 70 (above), 76, 77, 80; MSH 50; A. Rais, Delémont 23; RM 65, 79; Röm-German. Zentralmuseum, Mayence 22; Rosgarten-Museum, Constance 3, 4; Miss H. Schwab 10; Miss M. Sitterding 12; M. Yverdon 20.

The undermentioned figures were taken or adapted from the following works (listed in the Bibliography).

W. Drack, (ed.), 1968–74: 29, 31, 32, 37, 38, 40, 48, 49, 54, 56, 57, 59; M. Primas, 1970: 50, 52; O.-J. Bocksberger, 1964: 26.

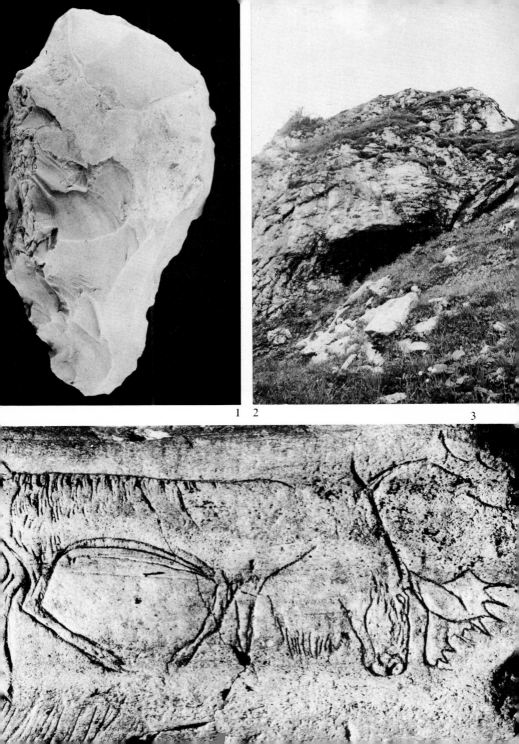

1   2   3

4

5

6

9

10

11

12

13

14

15

16

19

20

21

22

23

26

27

28

29

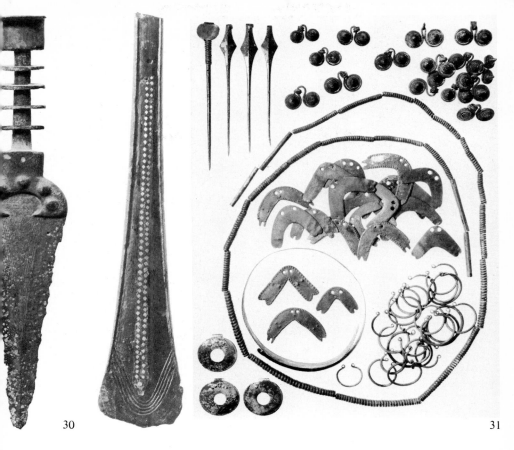

30 31

32

34

35

33

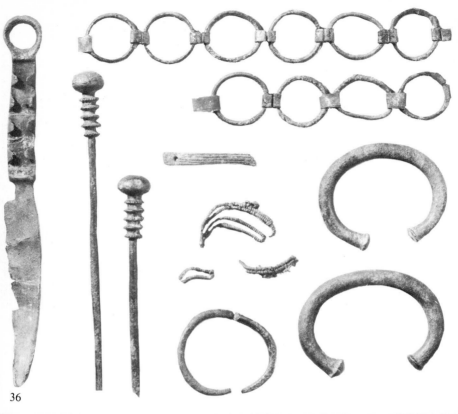

36

37

38

39

40

41

42

43

44

45

46

47

48

49

50

51

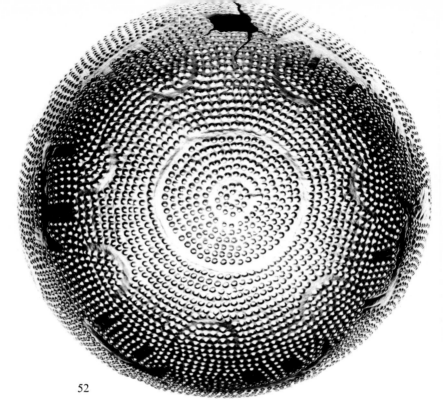

52

53

54

55

56

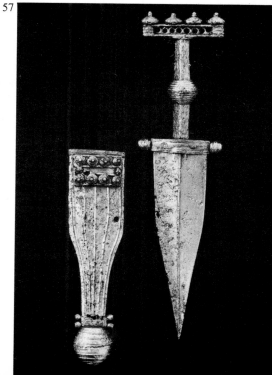

57

58

59

60

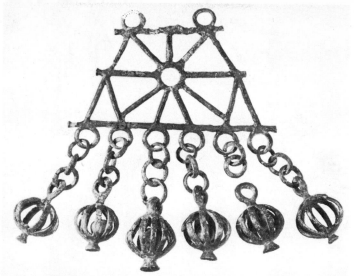

61

62

63

64

65

66

67

68

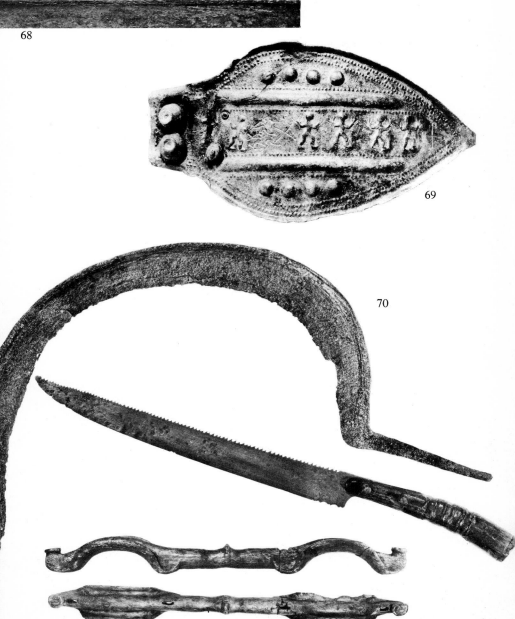

69

70

71

72

73

74

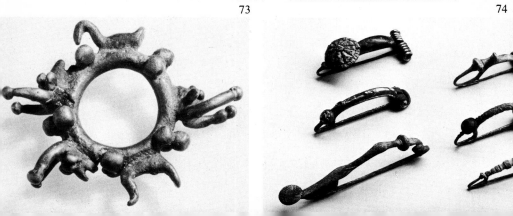

75

76

77

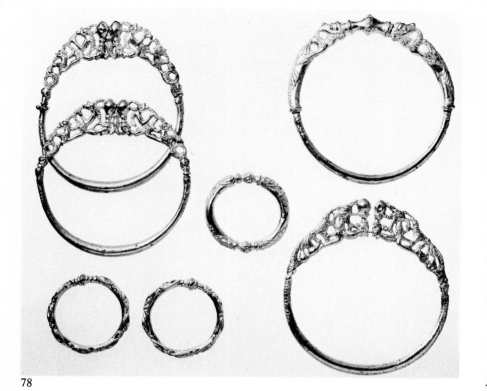

78

79

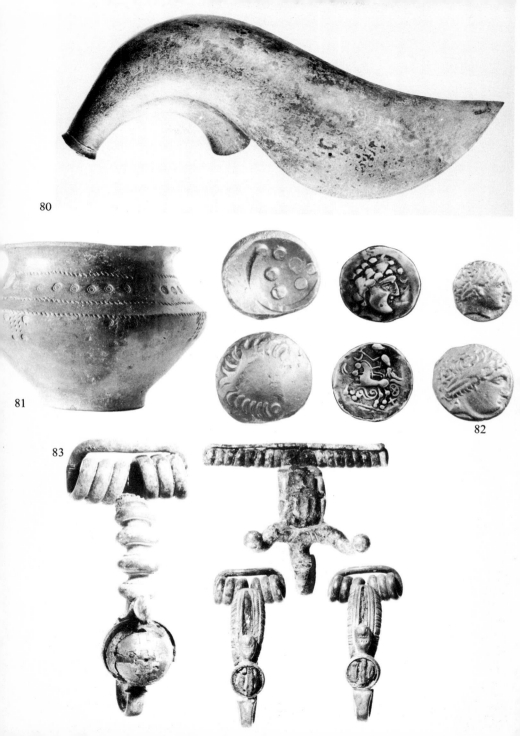

80

81

82

83

84

85

86

87

Notes on the Plates

1 Lower Palaeolithic; Acheulean; Pratteln BL; the first hand-axe found in Switzerland (1974). Length 18 cm. KMBL.

2 Middle Palaeolithic; Alpine Mousterian; Erlenbach BE, Chilchli cave, 1810 m.

3 Upper Palaeolithic; Late Magdalenian; Thayngen SH, Kesslerloch cave; unrolled photograph of a reindeer engraved on a shaft-straightener. Max. length of animal 8.2 cm.

4 Upper Paleolithic; Late Magdalenian; Thayngen SH, Kesslerloch cave; musk ox carved out of a reindeer antler. Length 6.2 cm.

5 Upper Palaeolithic; Late Magdalenian; Oensingen SO, Risliberg cave; ibex engraved on a 9.2-cm bone. KMSO.

6 Mesolithic; Nenzlingen BE; Birsmatten rockshelter; Tardenoisian level; engraved fragment of a rib. Length 5.8 cm.

7 Epipalaeolithic and Mesolithic, Sauveterrian and Tardenoisian; Nenzlingen BE, Birsmatten rockshelter after excavation.

8 Middle Neolithic; Egolzwil culture; Egolzwil LU, Egolzwil 3 settlement; typical pottery. Left: bottle-like receptacle with three handles (ht. 34 cm); bottom right: pot (ht. 16.4 cm); top right: imported beaker from the Rössen culture (ht. 9.2 cm).

9 Middle Neolithic; Cortaillod culture; Egolzwil LU, Egolzwil 4 settlement; foundation of a house with hearth on loam, during excavation (1954).

10 Middle Neolithic; Cortaillod culture; Thielle-Wavre NE; rivershore dwelling of Pont-de-Thielle; remains of a house and palisade.

11 Middle Neolithic; Cortaillod culture; Zurich lake-dwelling; pottery (partly reconstructed).

12 Middle Neolithic; Cortaillod culture; Chavanne-le-Chêne VD, Vallon des Vaux; rock-engraving.

13 Middle Neolithic in the Alps; Saint-Léonard VS; part of the complex of pits hollowed out of recent loess, between two low rocky slopes: in the background, the Rhône valley and the rocky hills of Sion.

14 Middle Neolithic in the Alps; Sion VS, rue des Collines; double alignment of menhirs just discovered under 4 m of Sionne alluvium: some menhirs are engraved (the alignment is now reconstructed a further few hundred metres).

15 Middle Neolithic in the Alps; Collombey-Muraz VS; Barmaz I; part of the cemetery: two cists, remaining lateral slab of a third cist, and two crouched corpses in the earth (which are older).

16 Middle Neolithic in the Alps; Collombey-Muraz VS; Barmaz II. Part of the cemetery (see fig. 13).

17 Middle Neolithic; Pfyn culture; typical pottery from the cantons ZH and TG. Left to right: from Zurich, Rentenanstalt; Uitikon ZH (ht. 13.5 cm); Zurich, Wollishofen; and (right and second right) Gachnang TG, Egelsee.

18 Late Neolithic; Horgen culture; Zurich,

Utoquai; typical pottery. Ht. of pot 3rd from right *c.* 30 cm.

19 Late Neolithic; Auvernier culture; Auvernier NE; comb made of withes and wood. Ht. 8 cm.

20 Late Neolithic; Corded Ware culture; Yverdon VD; typical pottery. Ht. 19.5 cm.

21 Late Neolithic in the Alps; Sion VS, Petit Chasseur; slabs of two tombs cut into anthropomorphic stelae. Left: from dolmen M VI, built before the arrival of the Beaker folk; the stele shows two stages of engraving (see fig. 22, 2b c); ht. 1.26 m. Right from cist M II; the head has been cut away; note the bent left arm; ht. 0.67 m.

22 Late Neolithic in the Alps; Bell Beaker culture; Sion VS, Petit Chasseur; beaker (reconstructed) from dolmen M I. Ht. 15.6 cm.

23 Neolithic lake dwelling; Lüscherz Locras BE, lake of Bienne. The double line of piles between the palisade and the present bushy shore was originally interpreted as the remains of a foot bridge; with the new interpretation of lake dwellings as sea shore settlements the piles can be regarded as the remains of a track crossing the damp ground.

24 Late Neolithic in the Alps; Bell Beaker culture; Sion VS, Petit Chasseur; dolmen M XI during excavation (1973). The roof slab was broken during the Early Bronze Age. The entrance is blocked by a small vertical slab partially concealed behind a heap of stones. All the slabs are engraved stelae. Scale: 1 m.

25 Late Neolithic in the Alps; Bell Beaker culture; Sion VS, Petit Chasseur; the earliest filling of the dolmen M XI: disturbed skeletons (with ornaments). Near the centre: white arrow pointing North and scale of 0.10 m.

26 Early Bronze Age in the Alps; Fellers GR, Muota; large discoïdal head of a giant pin. Total length of pin 85 cm; horizontal diameter of head 15.4 cm. RM.

27 Early Bronze Age in the Alps; Sion VS, Petit Chasseur; dolmen I; large coarse pot giving proof of the re use of the dolmen built by the Beaker folk. Ht. 39.5 cm.

28 Early Bronze Age in the Alps; Fellers GR, Muota; the wooded hill was occupied during the Early, Middle Bronze, and Iron Ages.

29 Early Bronze Age in the Alps; Cazis GR, Cresta; rock dwelling, foundations of two houses with hearth. At right, narrow path. Above the large hearth, scale of 1 m.

30 Early Bronze Age; Thoune Thun BE, Renzenbühl, objects from grave 1 (of a prince?). Left: bronze dagger (length 22.4 cm); right: axe (24 cm). Note on the axe the double row of gold ornamentation, incrusted in a copper band.

31 Early Bronze Age south of the Alps; Castione TI, Arbedo; hoard (of a merchant?) composed of 67 bronze ornaments: pins of two types, diadem, spiral tubes (reconstructed as necklace), pendants of various types. Length of longest pin 18.6 cm.

32 Middle Bronze Age; Weiningen ZH; barrow 3, grave 2; anklets and perforated pins. Length of longest pin 17.4 cm.

33 Middle Bronze Age; level of the fine ribbed pins; Thun Thoune BE, Allmend; rapier: the handle is finely engraved. Length 7.3 cm.

34 Beginning of Late Bronze Age; Mels phase; Wiedlisbach BE; excised pot seen from below, in the tradition of the Middle Bronze Age. Diameter 13.5 cm.

35 Beginning of Late Bronze Age; Vuadens FR; pottery found in a grave (under a

Roman villa). Ht. of largest receptacle 19.5 cm.

36 Beginning of Late Bronze Age; Binningen phase; Binningen BL; furniture from a female grave, including knife (length 23.5 cm), typical pins, armlets, fragments of an ornamental chain, etc.

37 Beginning of Late Bronze Age; Binningen phase; Binningen BL; gold-sheet belt ornament from female grave (as plate 36). Length 11 cm.

38 End of Late Bronze Age; Zug-Zoug, Sumpf; log-house in the upper level of the lake-dwelling (2.50 × 2.60 m).

39 Late Bronze Age; Zurich, Alpenquai; stone mould for a sickle and a knife. Breadth 24.2 cm.

40 Late Bronze Age; Zug-Zoug, Sumpf; pot with a variety of decoration: the holes in the neck were intended to receive coloured threads. Ht. 22 cm.

41 Late Bronze Age; Zurich, Alpenquai and (left) Grandson VD, Corcelettes. Black varnished pottery, imitating metal receptacles. Ht. of middle pot 10.5 cm.

42 End of Late Bronze Age; Zurich, Wollishofen and Alpenquai; typical pottery. Ht. of largest vessel 18.7 cm.

43 End of Late Bronze Age; Zurich, Wollishofen and Grosser Hafner; decorated plates (diameter of one at left 18.4 cm).

44 End of Late Bronze Age; Auvernier NE, lake-dwelling; remains of large basket made with withes of many colours. Diameter of base 15 cm.

45 Late Bronze Age; Zurich, Alpenquai (left) and Wollishofen; clay moon or horned figures ('horn-shaped fire-dogs'). Width of left figure 22 cm.

46 Late Bronze Age in upper Rhine valley; Melaun culture; Oberriet SG, Montlingerberg; typical pot. Ht. 16.5 cm.

47 Late Bronze Age in upper Rhine valley; Oberriet SG, Montlingerberg; stone

foundations of a rampart made of beams and earth.

48 Protohistoric rock-engravings in the Alps; Sils-im-Domleschg GR, Carschenna, rock II.

49 Late Bronze Age; Zurich, Alpenquai; ritual ornithomorphic pot. The hollow figure is ornamented with engraved lines filled with white lime paste or with coloured threads. Length 16 cm.

50 Early Hallstatt; Hemishofen SH, barrow 10; painted and engraved pottery. Breadth 35 cm.

51 Late Hallstatt; Posieux FR, Châtillon-sur-Glâne; large fibula.

52 End of Early or beginning of Late Hallstatt; Zurich, Altstetten; gold bowl, seen from below, embossed with dots delineating sun, moon, hound and hare motifs. Found in 1906, probably in the vicinity of a previously destroyed chieftain's barrow. Diameter 25 cm. Weight 910 g.

53 End of Early or beginning of Late Hallstatt; Ins-Anet BE; Grossholz chariot barrow; gold sphere decorated with granules and twisted gold wire. Diameter of sphere 1.2 cm.

54 End of Early or beginning of Late Hallstatt; Jegenstorf BE, barrow *im Hurst*; gold ornament. Diameter of sphere 1.2 cm.

55 Early Hallstatt; Ins-Anet BE, Grossholz chariot-barrow; fragments of the leather harness (with bronze studs) of a horse. Length of longest piece *c.* 36 cm.

56 Late Hallstatt; Echarlens FR; winged scabbard's chape. Max. breadth 8.5 cm.

57 Late Hallstatt; Estavayer-le-Lac FR (lake of Neuchâtel); iron dagger and scabbard. Length of dagger 24.2 cm.

58 Late Hallstatt; Meikirch BE, Grächwil barrow; bronze hydria with the figure of 'Oriental Artemis' surrounded by animals. From Greater Greece (presumably

from a workshop at Taranto); dated 580–570 BC. Ht. of vessel 50 cm.

59 Late Hallstatt or Early La Tène; Stallikon ZH, Uetliberg; part of the handle of an Attic crater with red figures. Maximum breadth 9.8 cm.

60 Hallstatt south of the Alps; Arbedo TI, Castione; pottery with black neck and foot, and a lattice pattern painted *a stralucido* on the belly. Ht. 25 cm.

61 Late Hallstatt; Subingen SO; chest ornament with bells found in a barrow. Length of lower horizontal shaft 10 cm.

62 Late Hallstatt; Bofflens VD; part ($\frac{3}{5}$) of a sheet-bronze woman's belt with repoussé frieze of human and geometrical motifs. Length 22 cm.

63 Late Hallstatt; Subingen SO; chest or ventral ornament found in a barrow. Diameter *c.* 15 cm.

64 Early La Tène; Andelfingen ZH; female grave; fibulae, armlets and rings. Breadth of largest fibula 11.2 cm.

65 Hallstatt in the Alps; Felsberg GR (near Tamins); painted and excised pottery. Diameter 20.5 cm.

66 End of Early La Tène; Saint-Sulpice VD; female grave from the cemetery; two-colour glass pendants in form of masks, of Punic origin. Ht. of piece at right 3.9 cm.

67 Early La Tène; Dietikon ZH; grave of a rich young woman. The furniture consists of 27 ornaments (16 fibulae, 5 arm and ankle-rings, 3 finger-rings, etc.). Exhibited in the Swiss National Museum.

68 Middle La Tène; Port BE; part of a sword blade with stamp (two ibex and tree) and owner's name engraved: KOPICIOC = KORISIOS. Length of name 1.5 cm.

69 Hallstatt south of the Alps; Giubiasco TI; belt garniture in sheet-bronze, with

human figures in repoussé and engraved zoomorphic and other motifs. Ht. 13 cm.

70 Middle La Tène; Marin-Epagnier NE, La Tène. Above: saw-knife and balanced sickle (length of saw 34 cm); below: yoke (length 116 cm).

71 Middle La Tène; Berne canton; gold, bronze and silver rings from Schalunen, Moetschwil and Berne-Aaregg. Diameter of left ring 7.8 cm.

72 Middle La Tène; Berne canton; glass armrings from Berne-Wylerfeld, Berne-Muristalden, Münsingen (two) and Moetschwil.

73 Middle La Tène; Port BE; small ring (amulet?) decorated with spheres, bulls and birds. Internal diameter 2.3 cm.

74 Middle La Tène; Münsingen BE, Rain; fibulae decorated with enamel, coral and bone.

75 Middle La Tène in the Alps; Leukerbad-Loëche-les-Bains VS; silver ring with hollow moving part. Diameter 8 cm.

76 Middle La Tène; Marin-Epagnier NE, La Tène; ornamented scabbards. Left: ornamental parts of a scabbard (serpentine motifs); the missing unornamented part is damaged (breadth of upper rim 4.5 cm). Right: horse-like motif in relief (maximum breadth 5.5 cm).

77 Middle La Tène; Marin-Epagnier NE, La Tène; a small sample of the spears found in the river Thièle. Length of spear at right: 34.5 cm.

78 Early La Tène in the Alps; Erstfeld UR; hoard of golden jewellery. Diameter of torque at bottom right 15 cm.

79 La Tène in the Alps; Ramosch GR, Mottata; stone foundations of a house. Sections of logs were put in the observed post-holes.

80 Middle La Tène; Marin-Epagnier NE, La Tène; bronze helmet-wing, or a bull's

ear used as a standard (?). Length 20 cm.

81 La Tène in the Alps; Tamins GR; pottery from a grave. Ht. 12 cm.

82 Middle La Tène; coins. Left: Aarberg BE; gold stater of *Regenbogenschüsselchen* type; weight 7.5 g. Centre: Sursee LU; quarterstater. Bottom right: Stäfa ZH; gold half-stater. Top right: Stäfa ZH; quarterstater. Diameter of piece at left 1.8 cm.

83 Middle La Tène south of the Alps; Giubiasco TI; enamelled fibulae with human masks or bull-horns. Length of longest fibula 11 cm.

84 La Tène south of the Alps; Lepontic inscriptions. Left: Davesco TI, Soragno (ht. *c.* 1.90 m). Transcription: 'TISIVI: PIVOTIALVI : PALA'; Stele for Tisios: Pivotialos (= son of Pivotios).

'SLANIAI : VERKALAI : PALA'; Stele of Slania: Verkala (= daughter of Verkos). Right: Stabio TI: 'MINVKV : KOMONEOS'; Minuku (and?) Komoneos (or: son of Komonos).

85 Early La Tène south of the Alps (Golasecca III); Arbedo TI, Cerinesca; beakers, one with an engraved mark of ownership. Ht. of left beaker 11.6 cm.

86 La Tène south of the Alps. Left: ceramic imitation from Bellinzona TI, Galbisio; right: bronze oenochoë (*Schnabelkanne*) from Arbedo TI, Castione-Molinazzo (ht. 26 cm).

87 Late La Tène south of the Alps; Giubiasco TI. Left: bronze helmet of Etruscan type (max. diameter 26.5 cm); right: iron helmet of Celtic type.

Bibliography

ABBREVIATIONS

ANTIQUA   Antiqua, Veröffentlichungen der SGU, Basle, 1973–

ASA   Anzeiger für Schweizerische Altertumskunde – Indicateur d'Antiquités suisses. Zurich, 1868–1938; NF, Neue Folge, 1899–1938

ASAG   Archives suisses d'Anthropologie générale, Geneva, 1914–

HELVETIA ANTIQUA   Helvetia Antiqua, Festschrift Emil Vogt, Beiträge zur Prähistorie und Archäologie der Schweiz, Zurich, 1966

HA   Helvetia Archaeologica, Archäologie in der Schweiz. Mitteilungsblatt der SGU, Zurich, 1970–

JBHM   Jahrbuch des Bernischen Historischen Museums in Bern. Abteilung für Ur- und Frühgeschichte, 1920–

JbSGU   Jahresbericht, then: Jahrbuch der SGU, 1908–

JHVFL   Jahrbuch des Historischen Vereins für das Fürstentum Liechtenstein, Vaduz, 1, 1901–

JSLMZ   Jahresbericht des Schweizerischen Landesmuseums in Zürich, 1892–

MAGZ   Mitteilungen der Antiquarischen Gesellschaft in Zürich, 1841–

MONOGR.   Monographien zur Ur- und Frühgeschichte der Schweiz (SGU), 1937–72

REPERTORIUM   Repertorium der Ur- und Frühgeschichte des Schweiz (SGU), 1955–60 (French translation except Heft 5): Répertoire de Préhistoire et d'Archéologie de la Suisse (SSP), 1958–63

SCHRIFTEN   Schriften des Instituts für Ur- und Frühgeschichte der Schweiz (SGU), 1944–71

SGU   Schweizerische Gesellschaft für Urgeschichte (since 1966: und Frühgeschichte). SSP: Société suisses de Préhistoire

US   Ur-Schweiz – La Suisse primitive, 1937–69

ZAK   Zeitschrift für Schweizerische Archäologie und Kunstgeschichte, Basle, 1939–

EARLY GENERAL WORKS

BONSTETTEN, G. DE., Recueil d'Antiquités suisses. Berne, 1855. Supplément . . . , Second supplément. Lausanne, 1860 and 1867.

HEIERLI, J., *Urgeschichte der Schweiz.* Zurich, 1901.

REINERTH, H., *Die jüngere Steinzeit der Schweiz.* Augsburg, 1926.

SCHENK, A., *La Suisse préhistorique. Le Paléolithique et le Néolithique.* Lausanne, 1912.

TSCHUMI, O. (ed.), *Urgeschichte der Schweiz.* I. *Die Steinzeit.* Frauenfeld, 1949.

MODERN GENERAL WORKS

DRACK, W. and SCHIB, K., *Illustrierte Geschichte der Schweiz*. I. *Urgeschichte, römische Zeit und Mittelalter*. Zurich, 2nd ed., 1971.

DRACK, W. (ed.), *Ur- und frühgeschichtliche Archäologie der Schweiz*. I. *Die ältere und mittlere Steinzeit;* II. *Die Jungsteinzeit;* III. *Die Bronzezeit;* IV. *Die Eisenzeit*. Basle, SGU, 1968, 1969, 1971, 1974.

VOGT, E., Histoire I. Epoques préhistoriques, in: *Atlas der Schweiz – Atlas de la Suisse – Atlante della Svizzera*. Wabern, 1965– (1968, pl. 19).

—Urgeschichte, in: *Handbuch der Schweizer Geschichte*, I. Zurich, 1972.

THE LAND

HANTKE, R., Das Quartär der Schweiz, in: *The Quaternary of the World*. New York, 1962.

HOFFMAN, G. W. (ed.), *A geography of Europe*. London, 2nd ed., 1963. (Switzerland: 443–53).

REGIONAL STUDIES

AMREIN, W., *Urgeschichte des Vierwaldstätter Sees und der Innerschweiz*. Aarau, 1939. (LU, NW, OW, SZ, UR, ZG)

BERGER, L., Die Anfänge Basels, in: *Basel, eine illustrierte Stadtgeschichte*. Basle, 1969. (BS)

BLONDEL, L., Le développement urbain de Genève à travers les siècles. *Cahiers de Préhistoire et d'Archéologie* 3. Geneva – Nyon, 1946. (GE)

BURKART, W., Die urgeschichtliche Besiedlung Alträtiens. *Bündner Schulblatt* 13, Chur, 1953. (GR)

CRIVELLI, A., *Atlante preistorico e storico della Svizzera italiana*. I. Bellinzona, 1943. (TI)

GUYAN, W. U., *Erforschte Vergangenheit*. Schaffhausen, 1971. (SH)

HEIERLI, J., *Archaeologische Karte des Kantons Zürich*. Zurich, 1894. (ZH)

—Archäologische Karte des Kantons Aargau. Aarau, 1899. (AG)

—Urgeschichte Graubündens. *MAGZ* 21, 1903. (GR)

—Die archäologische Karte des Kantons Solothurn. Soleure, 1905. (SO)

KELLER, F., *Archaeologische Karte der Ostschweiz*. Zurich, 2nd ed., 1874. (AR, IR, SG, TG)

—Beilage zur archäologischen Karte der Ostschweiz. Frauenfeld, 1873.

KELLER-TARNUZZER, K. and REINERTH, H., *Urgeschichte des Thurgaus*. Frauenfeld, 1925. (TG)

MILLOTTE, J.-P., Le Jura et les plaines de Saône aux âges des métaux. *Annales littéraires de l'Université de Besançon*, 59, *Archéologie* 16, Paris, 1963.

MONTANDON, R., *Genève des origines aux invasions barbares*. Geneva, 1922. (GE)

PEISSARD, N., *Carte archéologique du canton de Fribourg*. Fribourg, 1941. (FR)

SAUTER, M.-R., Préhistoire du Valais des origines aux temps mérovingiens. (+2 supplements to the archaeological inventory). *Vallesia*, Sion, 5, 1950; 10, 1955; 15, 1960. (VS)

—Les premiers millénaires, in: *Histoire de Genève*. Toulouse-Lausanne, 1974. (GE)

SCHWAB, H. and MÜLLER, R., *Le passé du Seeland sous un jour nouveau. Les niveaux des lacs du Jura*. Fribourg, 1973. (BE, FR, NE, VD)

SPECK, M. and J., Ur- und Frühgeschichte *(Das*

Bibliography

Buch vom Lande Zug, Zuger Festgabe, Zentenarfeier 1952). Zug, 1952. (ZG)

TSCHUMI, O., *Urgeschichte des Kantons Bern.* Berne, 1953. (BE)

VIOLLIER, D., *Carte archéologique du canton de Vaud.* Lausanne, 1927. (VD)

VOUGA, D., *Préhistoire du pays de Neuchâtel.* Neuchâtel, 1943. (NE)

ZÜRCHER, A., Urgeschichtliche und römerzeitliche Fundstellen Graubündens. *Schriftenreihe des Rätischen Museums*, Chur, 1976. (GR)

PALAEOLITHIC AND MESOLITHIC

ANDRIST, D., FLÜKIGER, W. and ANDRIST, A., Das Simmental zur Steinzeit. *Acta Bernensia* 3, Berne, 1964.

BÄCHLER, E., Das alpine Paläolithikum der Schweiz. *Monographien* 2, Basle, 1940.

BANDI, H. G., *Die Schweiz zur Rentierzeit.* Frauenfeld, 1947.

BANDI, H. G. (dir.), Birsmatten-Basisgrotte, eine mittelsteinzeitliche Fundstelle im unteren Birstal. *Acta Bernensia* 1, Berne, 1963.

DUBOIS, A. and STEHLIN, H. G., La grotte de Cotencher, station moustérienne. *Mémoires de la Société paléontologique suisse,* Basle, 1933.

EGLOFF, M., La Baume d'Ogens, gisement épipaléolithique du Plateau vaudois. Note préliminaire. *JbSGU* 52, 1965.

—Les gisements préhistoriques de Baulmes (Vaud). *JbSGU* 53, 1966–67.

FEUSTEL, R., Remarques sur le Magdalénien suisse. *ASAG* 26, 1967.

GIGON, R., La grotte préhistorique du Bichon (La Chaux-de Fonds, Neuchâtel). *ASAG* 21, 1956.

SARASIN, F., Die steinzeitlichen Fundstellen des Birstals zwischen Basel und Delsberg. *Denkschriften der Schweiz. Naturforschenden Gesellschaft* 54, 1918.

SCHMID, E., Höhlenforschung und Sedimentanalyse. Ein Beitrag zur Datierung des Alpinen Paläolithikums. *Schriften* 13, 1958.

SONNEVILLE-BORDES, D. DE., Le Paléolithique supérieur en Suisse. *L'Anthropologie* 67, Paris, 1963.

WYSS, R., Beiträge zur Typologie der Paläolithisch-mesolithischen Übergangsformen im schweizerischen Mittelland. *Schriften* 9, 1953.

THE NEOLITHIC

BAER, A., Die Michelsberger Kultur. *Monographien* 12, 1959. (Critique by J. Driehaus in *Germania* 39, 1961).

BANDI, H. G. and MÜLLER-BECK, Hj. (ed.), Seeberg, Burgäschi-Süd. 8 Teile (3, 4, 5 and 6 soon published) *Acta Bernensia* 2, Berne, 1963–73.

BOCKSBERGER, O. J., Nouvelles recherches au Petit-Chasseur à Sion (Valais, Suisse). *JbSGU* 56, 1971.

DRIEHAUS, J., *Die Altheimer-Gruppe und das Jungneolithikum in Mitteleuropa.* Mayence, 1960.

GALLAY, A., Les stratigraphies de la Suisse et la structure du Néolithique d'Europe occidentale. *Sibrium*, Varese, 10, 1970 (German translation in *Germania* 49, 1971).

—Le Néolithique moyen du Jura et des plaines de la Saône. Contribution à l'étude des relations Chassey-Cortaillod-Michelsberg. Thesis Paris (in press: *Antiqua* 1976).

GUYAN, W. U., Die jungsteinzeitlichen Moordörfer im Weier bei Thayngen. *ZAK* 25, 1967.

ITTEN, M., Die Horgener Kultur *Monographien* 17, 1970.

LÜNING, J., Die Michelsberger Kultur. Ihre Funde in zeitlicher und räumlicher Gliederung. 48. *Bericht der Römische-Germanischen Kommission*, 1967.

MAUSER-GOLLER, K., Die relative Chronologie des Neolithikums in Südwestdeutschland und der Schweiz. *Schriften* 15, 1969.

REINERTH, H. and BOSCH, R., Das Grabhügel von Sarmenstorf. Ausgrabungen 1927. *ASA* 31, 1929.

SAUTER, M.-R., Sépultures à cistes du bassin du Rhône et civilisations palafittiques. *Sibrium*, Varese, 2, 1955.

—GALLAY, A. and CHAIX, L., Le Néolithique du niveau inférieur de Petit-Chasseur à Sion, Valais. *JbSGU* 56, 1971.

SITTERDING, M., Le Vallon des Vaux. Rapports culturels et chronologiques. *Monographien* 20, 1972.

STRAHM, C., Die Gliederung der schnurkeramischen Kultur in der Schweiz. *Acta Bernensia* 6, 1971.

—Les fouilles d'Yverdon. *JbSGU* 57, 1972–73.

VOGT, E., Geflechte und Gewebe der Steinzeit. *Monographien* 1, 1937.

—Der Stand der neolithischen Forschung in der Schweiz. *JbSGU* 51, 1964.

—Ein Schema des schweizerischen Neolithikums. *Germania* 45, 1967.

VOUGA, P., The oldest Swiss lake-dwellings. *Antiquity* 1, 1928.

—Classification du Néolithique lacustre suisse. *ASA* 31, 1929.

—Le Néolithique lacustre ancien. *Recueil des travaux*, Faculté des Lettres, Université de Neuchâtel, 1934.

WINIGER, J., Das Fundmaterial von Thayngen Weier im Rahmen der Pfyner Kultur. *Monographien* 18, 1971.

WYSS, R., Anfänge des Bauerntums in der Schweiz. Die Egolzwiler Kultur (um 2700 v. Christ). *Aus dem Schweizerischen Landesmuseum* 12, Berne, 1959.

—Ein jungsteinzeitliches Hockergräberfeld mit Kollektivbestattungen bei Lenzburg, Kt. Aargau. *Germania* 45, 1967.

—Wirtschaft und Gesellschaft in der Jungsteinzeit. *Monographien zur Schweizer Geschichte* 6, Berne, 1973.

THE LAKE-DWELLINGS

GUYAN, W. U. (ed.), Das Pfahlbauproblem (see especially VOGT, E. Pfahlbaustudien). *Monographien* 11, 1955.

ISCHER, T., *Die Pfahlbauten des Bielersees.* Bienne, 1928.

KELLER, F., Die keltischen Pfahlbauten in den Schweizerseen. [Pfahlbauten, 1. Bericht]. *MAGZ* 9, 1854.

—*The lake dwellings of Switzerland and other parts of Europe* (translated and arranged by J. E. Lee). London, 1866.

PARET, O., *Le mythe des cités lacustres et les problèmes de la construction néolithique.* Paris, 1958.

Pfahlbauten. Bericht 1–12. (F. KELLER, 1–8; J. HEIERLI, 9; D. VIOLLIER, 10–12). *MAGZ*, 9, 1854; 12, 1858; 13, 1860; 14, 1861 and 1863; 15, 1866; 19, 1876; 20, 1879; 22, 1888; 29, 1924; 30, 1930.

REINERTH, H., Waren die vorgeschichtlichen Pfahlbauten Wasser- oder Landsiedlungen? *Die Erde* 3, 1925.

Bibliography

SAUTER, M./R., Quelques réflexions à propos du problème des palafittes. *Genava* n.s., 7, 1959.

TSCHUMI, O., RYTZ, W. and FAVRE, J., Sind die Pfahlbauten Trocken/ oder Wassersiedlungen gewesen? Ur/ und na/ turgeschichtliche Untersuchung. 18. *Be/ richt der Römisch/Germanischen Kommission*, 1928.

VIOLLIER, D., VOUGA, P., TSCHUMI, O. and RYTZ, W., Die Moor und Seesiedlun/ gen in der Ost/ und Zentralschweiz. Die Moor/ und Seesiedlungen in der West/ schweiz. Pfahlbauten, 11. Bericht. *MAGZ* 30, 6–7, 1930.

THE BRONZE AGE

BERSU, G., Das Wittnauer Horn im Kanton Aargau. *Monographien* 4, 1945.

BILL, J., Die Glockenbecherkultur und die frühe Bronzezeit im französischen Rhone/ becken und ihre Beziehungen zur Südwest/ schweiz. *Antiqua* 1, 1973.

BURKART, W., Crestaulta, eine bronzezeit/ liche Seidlung bei Surin in Lugnez. *Monographien* 5, 1946.

BOCKSBERGER, O./J., *Age du Bronze en Valais et dans le Chablais vaudois*. Thesis, University of Lausanne, 1964.

FISCHER, F., Die frühbronzezeitliche Ansied/ lung in der Bleiche bei Arbon, TG. *Schriften* 17, 1971.

FREI, B., Die Gliederung der Melauner Keramik. *ZAK* 15, 1954.

—Zeugen der älteren Urnenfelderzeit aus dem Bereich des oberen Alpenrheins. *Hel/ vetia Antiqua,* 1966.

GALLAY, A. and G., Le Jura et la séquence Néolithique récent – Bronze ancien. *ASAG* 33, 1968.

GALLAY, G., Das Ende der Frühbronzezeit im Schweizer Mittelland. *JbSGU* 56, 1971.

KIMMIG, W., Weiningen und Harthausen. Ein Beitrag zu hochbronzezeitlichen Bestat/ tungssitten im nordschweizerisch/ südwestdeutschen Raum. *Helvetia Antiqua,* 1966.

KRAFT, G., Die Stellung der Schweiz in/ nerhalb der bronzezeitlichen Kulturgrup/ pen Mitteleuropas. *ASA* 29, 1927; 30, 1928.

MILLOTTE, J./P., Une ancienne découverte de l'âge du Bronze à Genève. Le dépôt de la Maison Buttin en l'Ile. *ASAG* 38, 1974.

MUELLER/KARPE, H., Beiträge zur Chrono/ logie der Urnenfelderzeit nördlich und südlich der Alpen. *Römisch/Germanische Forschungen* 22, Berlin, 1959.

OSTERWALDER, C., Die mittlere Bronzezeit im schweizerischen Mittelland und Jura. *Monographien* 19, 1971.

SANGMEISTER, E., Die Sonderstellung der schweizerischen Frühbronzezeit/Kultur. *Helvetia Antiqua,* 1966.

SCHWAB, H., Prähistorische Kupferfunde aus dem Kanton Freiburg. *JbSGU* 55, 1970.

SITTERDING, M., Bourdonnette et Bois/de/ Vaux, deux complexes de l'âge du Bronze ancien [VD]. *Helvetia Antiqua,* 1966.

STRAHM, C., Renzenbühl und Ringoldswil. Die Fundgeschichte zweier frühbronzezeit/ lichen Komplexe. *JBHM* 45–46, 1965–66.

VOGT, E., Die Gliederung der schweizeris/ chen Frühbronzezeit. *Festschrift O. Tsch/ umi*. Frauenfeld, 1948.

ZINDEL, C., Felszeichnungen auf Cars/ chenna, Gemeinde Sils im Domleschg. *US* 32, 1968.

THE FIRST IRON AGE (HALLSTATT)

DRACK, W., Aeltere Eisenzeit der Schweiz. 1–3. Kanton Bern; 4. Die Westschweiz. *Materialhefte* 1–4, 1958–64.

—(Papers on typology, chronology and distribution of the archaeological material of the Hallstatt period in Switzerland). *ZAK* 18, 1958. *JbSGU* 52, 1965 to 55, 1970; 57, 1972–73.

FREI, B., MENGHIN, O., MEYER, E. and RISCH, E., Der heutige Stand der Räterforschung in geschichtlicher, sprachlicher und archäologischer Sicht. *JbSGU* 55, 1970, and *Schriftenreihe des Rätischen Museums, Chur*, 10, 1970.

GUYAN, W. U., Das Grabhügelfeld im Sankert bei Hemishofen [SH]. *Schriften* 8, 1951.

HEIERLI, J., Die Grabhügel von Unterlunkhofen, Kt. Aargau. *ASA* 7, 1905–06; 8, 1906.

—Die goldene Schüssel von Zürich. *ASA* 9, 1907.

HUNDT, H.-J., Technische Untersuchung eines hallstattzeitlichen Dolches von Estavayer-le-Lac [FR]. *JbSGU* 52, 1965.

KRÄMER, W., Prähistorische Brandopferplätze. *Helvetia Antiqua*, 1966.

PITTIONI, R., Grächwil und Vix handelsgeschichtlich gesehen. *Helvetia Antiqua*, 1966.

PRIMAS, M., Die südschweizerischen Grabfunde der älteren Eisenzeit und ihre Chronologie [TI, GR]. *Monographien* 16, 1970.

REINERTH, H. and BOSCH, R., Ein Grabhügel der Hallstattzeit von Seon im Kanton Aargau. *ASA* 35, 1933.

SARBACH, H., Das Eggli bei Spiez (Berner Oberland), eine Kultstätte der Urnenfelder- und Hallstattzeit. *JBHM* 41–42, 1961–62.

VIOLLIER, D. (and F. BLANC), (3 papers on barrows). *ASA* 12, 1910; 15, 1913; 16, 1914.

VOGT, E., Hügelgrab bei Dietikon, Kt. Zürich. *JSLMZ* 39, 1930.

—Osservazioni sulla necropoli di Cerinasca d'Arbedo [TI]. Munera (Raccolta di scritti in onore di A. Giussani), *Società Archeologica Comense*, 1944.

—Der Beginn der Eisenzeit in der Schweiz. *JbSGU* 40, 1949–50.

WIEDMER, J., Die Grabhügel bei Subingen [SO]. *ASA* 10, 1908.

THE SECOND IRON AGE (LA TÈNE)

ALLEN, D. F., The coins found at La Tène [NE]. (Actes du 4ᵉ Congrès internat. d'études celtiques, Rennes, 1971, vol. II.) *Etudes Celtiques* 13, 1973.

BERCHEM, D. VAN., Du portage au péage. Le rôle des cols transalpins dans l'histoire du Valais celtique. *Museum Helveticum* 13, 1956.

BERGER, L. and FURGER, A., Das spätkeltische Oppidum von Basel-Münsterhügel . . . – Der murus gallicus von 1971. *Archäologisches Korrespondenzblatt*, Mainz, 1972.

BURKART, W., Die Schnabelkanne von Castaneda [GR]. *ASA* 40, 1938.

CRIVELLI, A., Presentazione del ripostiglio d'un fonditore di bronzi dell' epoca del Ferro scoperto ad Arbedo [TI]. *Rivista di Studi liguri* 12, 1946.

—La necropoli di Ascona [TI]. *Sibrium*, Varese, 1, 1953–54.

Bibliography

FREI, B., Zu einigen ergänzten Gefässen der Schnellerkeramik. *JHVFL* 56, 1956.

—Urgeschichtliche Räter im Engadin und Rheintal. *JbSGU* 55, 1970.

GALLAY, A., Une tombe du second âge du Fer à Sion (Valais, Suisse). Méthode de fouille et interprétation. *L'Homme, hier et aujourd'hui. Recueil d'études en hommage à André Leroi-Gourhan.* Paris, 1973.

GRUAZ, J. and VIOLLIER, D., Le cimetière gaulois de Saint-Sulpice (Vaud). *ASA* 16, 1914; 17, 1915.

HILD, A. and MERHART, G. VON., Vor- und frühgeschichtliche Funde von Gutenberg-Balzers, 1932/33. *JHVFL* 33, 1933.

HODSON, F. R., La Tène cemetery at Münsingen-Rain [BE]. Catalogue and relative chronology. *Acta Bernensia* 5, 1968.

JACOBSTHAL, P. and LANGSDORFF, A., *Die Bronzeschnabelkannen.* Berlin, 1929.

MAJOR, E., Gallische Ansiedlung mit Gräberfeld bei Basel. Basle, 1940. (Completed by *JbSGU* 31, 1939, 74).

MÜLLER-BECK, H. and ETTLINGER, E., Die Besiedlung der Engehalbinsel in Bern auf Grund des Kenntnisstandes vom Februar des Jahres 1962. 43–4. *Bericht der Römisch-Germanischen Kommission,* 1962–63. Berlin, 1964.

NAEF, A., Le cimetière gallo-helvète de Vevey [VD]. *ASA* 3, 1901; 4, 1903.

NAVARRA, J. M. DE., *The finds from the site of La Tène. I. Scabbards and the swords found in them.* London, 1972.

PILLERI, G. and SCHWAB, H., Morphological structures in 2100-year old Celtic brains [Cornaux NE]. *Man* 5, 1970.

PRIMAS, M., Eine Bronzeschnabelkanne des Tessimer Typs aus Castaneda [GR]. *JbSGU* 54, 1968–69.

PÜMPIN, F., Spätgallische Töpferöfen in Sissach, Kanton Baselland. *Germania* 19, 1935.

RADDATZ, K., Zur Deutung der Funde von La Tène [NE]. *Offa* 11, 1952.

RUOFF, U., Eine Spätlatènesiedlung bei Marthalen [ZH]. *JbSGU* 51, 1964.

STÄHELIN, F., *Die Schweiz in römischer Zeit.* 3rd ed. Basle, 1948.

STORK, I., Neue Beobachtungen zum Gräberfeld Münsingen-Rain [BE]. *JbSGU* 57, 1972–73.

TRÜMPLER, D., BÉRARD, C. and SAUTER, M.-R., Tombes de La Tène C trouvées dans le village du Levron (commune de Vollèges, Valais). *ASAG* 22, 1957.

VIOLLIER, D., Le cimetière gallo-helvète d'Andelfingen (Zurich). *ASA* 17, 1912.

—Les 'bracelets valaisans'. *Genava* 7, 1929.

—*Les sépultures du second âge du Fer sur le Plateau suisse.* Geneva, 1916.

VOGT, E., La Tènegräber von Dietikon, Kanton Zürich. *JSLMZ* 60, 1951.

VOUGA, P., La Tène. *Monographie de la station . . .* Leipzig, 1923.

WYSS, R., Das Schwert des Korisios [Port, Nidau BE]. *JBMM* 34, 1954.

—*Funde der jüngeren Eisenzeit (470 bis Christi Geburt).* (From *Schweizerischen Landesmuseum* 8). Berne, 1957.

ADDENDUM

JEQUIER, J.-P. Le Moustérien alpin, révision critique. *Eburodunum II et Cahiers d'Archéologie romande,* 2, Yverdon, 1975.

WYSS, R. *Der Goldschatz von Erstfeld. Frühkeltischer Goldschmuck ans den Zentralpen,* Zurich, 1975.

Index

Index